SPECIAL EDUCATION BOOK

SPECIAL EDUCATION BOOK

A RESOURCE BOOK FOR TEACHERS AND OTHER PROFESSIONALS SERVICING STUDENTS WITH DISABILITIES

DR. MARLYN PANGATUNGAN

Charleston, SC
www.PalmettoPublishing.com

Special Education Book
Copyright © 2022 by Dr. Marlyn Pangatungan

First Edition

Paperback ISBN: 978-1-68515-706-7

Dedicated to my brother, Police Major Jodel Torregosa (deceased).

To my husband, Rey.
And to my children—Stacey, Samantha, and Blaise.

And to my mother, Adelaida Pacaldo Torregosa, and my siblings—
Glenda, Joel, Jonel, Jodel, Dandy, and Marlon.

And to a special grandmother of my children, Socorro Goncer Dupuis.

This book is dedicated to all special education teachers who choose to be exceptional in their profession and exercise their great interest and enthusiasm in teaching children with disabilities;

to those who desire to be called special education teachers—you are all called to be in this profession as you continue to fulfill the demands of teaching—and to all of you who have the warmest hearts and want to teach and touch the hearts of our students with disabilities.

This book should only be seen as an addendum to information already in schools. This is not a fixed resource as schools' needs vary. You may use the information gained from this book as an additional source of knowledge.

TABLE OF CONTENTS

ACKNOWLEDGMENTS

Whether through written work or in conversations with me, the following individuals directly or indirectly helped in the process and provided me with information; the Facebook Community of Special Education Teachers members; Socorro Dupuis; my husband; my children; and most of all, the one person who coached and mentored me and made me a better special education teacher, Mary Cain-Hale.

I acknowledge the comprehensive effort of the publishing company in editing my book.

As always, I am grateful to my family. My husband, Rey, spent quality time with my children while I wrote this book. My children—Stacey, Samantha, and Blaise—were unconditionally understanding that their mom was busy writing this book.

Thank you all. Because of you, I was able to do what I love to do, and I owe everything to you.

Marlyn Pangatungan, EdD
Shreveport, Louisiana
2022

FOREWORD

Leaving a country where culture and instruction were different and landing in a new country where the special education (a.k.a. SE) curriculum was much more structured and advanced was a total shock to me. I came to a brand-new place where everything in the classroom was quite exceptional, all technology was available for teachers' use, from computers to smart boards to Promethean boards, and materials and resources were free for educators to utilize in teaching—being able to make unlimited copies of worksheets is priceless. Now, I have a huge copier in my own classroom! Also, I was shocked at the culture and curriculum. Lessons were available for teachers to peruse and use for teaching. Teachers didn't have to rethink what to write in the lesson plan as it was already made available. Hands-on materials were everywhere, and each student had technology to use, especially during the pandemic. Teachers' needs in the classroom were fulfilled by the school and district. Teachers have everything they need in the classroom.

This was way different than what I experienced before. Then, the students were taller and bigger than me. I was a bit intimidated by their physical appearance at first, but as I gained teaching experience, I became acculturated and acclimated to the school system. Also, in the beginning, other teachers were a bit distant, but the more we got to know each other, we laughed, talked, discussed, collaborated and shared so many things about life and our teaching experiences.

I remembered my first year as a special education teacher (SET). I was full of questions, nervous, had no clue what to do, and did not know where I was heading, but I was determined to do my job. I was first assigned to be an inclusion teacher in a middle school setting. Not only did I do inclusion support for my students but also the documentation and the paperwork of an inclusion teacher. There were many things I needed to do aside from servicing my students. I had to deal with the academic side of providing support to my students and at the same time ensure that I filled out all of the documentation that needed to be submitted to the special education department. It had to be done within the timeline provided. Individualized education plan (IEP) meetings and amendment meetings frequently occurred. Inclusion documentation logs needed to be completed daily, and communication to parents was constant as well.

I did it with little knowledge and information until an instructional specialist assigned to our school came and did a thorough orientation focused on what a newly hired SET should know in terms of writing IEPs, meetings, related services, writing progress reports, forms, and servicing students in the classroom. It was the longest three hours of my special education teaching life, but I was grateful because I was educated, informed, and able to learn the things I needed to know to effectively and efficiently service my students.

Aside from the in-services at school, there were plenty of special education professional development opportunities (PDs) offered at the school district level. I attended almost all of the PDs not only because they were part of the content learning units (CLUs) to renew teaching certificates but also because I wanted to learn as much as possible to serve my students better. It was part of my professional growth. There were things that I did not learn during my special education college courses that I learned through PDs and teaching experiences. I grabbed every opportunity to take PDs offered at the special education department.

The things I learned from the PDs I used with my students and in my teaching in the classroom. There were many challenges in the classroom—behavior, personality, ability, social skills and learning. These challenges, together with the students' skill deficits, came to light as you learned to get to know each child. Being a SET is not just being in the classroom; it is more of understanding the whole child—they might be middle-school-aged but have personal struggles at home, at school, and in the community, and their academic performance might not at all reflect their functional abilities. Students came to school with different concerns and issues—some slept at their desks, some did not submit homework, some did not have food to eat, some had behavioral issues triggered at home, and some had already experienced long-term issues in their personal lives. What was most challenging was that the teachers were ready for students to learn yet some of the students were not yet ready to learn on that day—or teachers were not prepared to teach students what they needed. It was a constant struggle in the beginning as I tried to understand my students' behavior and abilities, but I endured these challenges. Now my teaching life is much better.

I remembered my very first IEP meeting. The IEP I knew from where I had come from and from my research proved totally different from what I was seeing at my school. My instructional specialist sat on the computer as she revised almost all of the IEP information I typed. She was very accommodating and gave me advice on rewording, changing, excising, and adding more details to the IEPs. I was honest with her, telling her it was my very first IEP as a special education teacher at that school, but that very first IEP meeting was nonetheless a success.

The most important thing was that every day I learned something new—in the classroom as a support provider and as a SET writing IEPs for my students with disabilities. It was both a challenge and excitement that I was able to endure, and my tolerance was greater than I thought it would be during my first year as a SET.

The next year came; I had a new instructional specialist. I was blessed to have her as she became my mentor in SE. She coached me every step of the way, and I learned so much from her. I became coachable. I was mentored. I seized every opportunity for guidance. I opened my mind to the possibility of learning everything she was pouring in. She may not know it, but I owe much of what I know about special education today to her. She taught me how to prepare for an IEP conference correctly, how to complete paperwork after an IEP, how to amend an IEP, how to deal with people, how to be myself, and how to handle issues during difficult situations—she religiously guided me as we went through our daily tasks at school. She was my defender when someone would underestimate me. We worked together to get the special education paperwork done on time. We conducted house visits when parents could not come to the school. We went above and beyond our job description. We just had a great team.

It is important that you take advantage of the people who would like to help you become successful as a SET. It is not always the case that someone will take the time to help, support, coach, or mentor another. When you know that someone is there to help you, seize on it because the learnings you will gain will forever be ingrained in your heart and mind. Have a positive attitude toward learning because the steps may not be smooth all the time, but the end result of the experience is wonderful and worth the effort.

Almost thirteen years later, I became the one who was mentoring and coaching new SETs voluntary and nonvoluntary, at my school. I paid it forward just because of that one person who believed in me and my abilities. If we know something, it is our responsibility to share that knowledge. Be grateful and giving at the same time.

I learned certain things upfront. Theory and practice were distantly real. I grabbed every PD opportunity because I wanted to learn. I had terrific instructional specialists who worked, mentored, and molded me into being a better SET. I learned so much from them. So, I thought to myself, why not pay it forward with other new SETs? Why not help them learn things they did not learn during college courses? Why not share with them my firsthand experience of going through struggles and challenges as a new SET and overcoming to be a better SET because someone coached me to become better? Why not impart to them the things I learned so together we can serve our students with disabilities better?

I hope that through this book, every hired SET will learn something from all of the information I share as this is my firsthand experience. Also, I hope that even those veteran teachers will learn something from this book. This can serve as a refresher. It is also applicable to those aspiring to become SETs.

Good luck on your journey as a SET. Every day is different. It can be wonderful or challenging. No matter what kind of day it is, remember, you are called to service—to serve students with disabilities because you see opportunities and exceptional abilities despite their disabilities. You chose to become SET because you see a purpose for each one of the students you are providing support to. You chose to bring miracles to their lives, one individual at a time.

And to the veterans, we are lifelong learners, so enjoy learning as you refresh, recall, relearn. Overall, this book is for all of us so that we can serve our students with disabilities (SWDs) with gratitude, love, care, respect, and kindness. We are all unique, and we belong to each other.

I wish you all good luck on your special education teaching journey.

INTRODUCTION

*No Child Left Behind requires states and school districts
to ensure that all students are learning and are reaching
their highest potential. Special education students should
not be left out of these accountability mechanisms.*
—Dianne Feinstein

Personalize learning for all.

This book is meant to serve as a resource for educators to assist in their understanding of how to support students with special needs in the classroom. Both regular and special education settings are addressed. This book should be used as a resource, not a strict set of rules that must be followed. However, some nonnegotiable practices required by federal and state regulations/rules are included.

Furthermore, this book focuses on the different aspects of special education laws, regulations, guidelines, diverse and inclusive instruction, paraprofessionals, and the inclusive classroom. While this book does not explicitly address these tasks and job responsibilities, SETs, paraprofessionals (the teacher support in the classroom), other related service personnel, aspiring SETs, and any individual who wishes to learn about special education must know the legal mandates and information so as to serve our students better and meet their individual needs. The underlying tasks and details must not be undervalued or disregarded; however, how these tasks should be carried out needs to be determined locally based on a specific student's needs and thus cannot be comprehensively addressed within this book.

While there is no perfect guide that can answer every question teachers may have, this book is intended to spark dialogues within schools or local education agencies. Decisions are communicated at the local level with the idea that any support associated with students who receive special education services be individualized to each student, classroom setting, and even class period, as well as the type of instruction being provided (whole group, small group, co-teaching, and other types of classroom instruction).

In other words, the information shared in this book serves as a guide and should be adapted and modified to fit your school's needs. It can also serve as a learning platform for those parents who are home-schooling their children. No matter how you use this book, I hope that you find the information useful, relatable, and valuable to you. I thank you in advance for supporting me by purchasing this book.

CHAPTER 1: OVERVIEW OF SPECIAL EDUCATION

Education is the most powerful weapon which
you can use to change the world.
—Nelson Mandela

As a special education teacher (SET), you already know that you cannot release just any identifying information about your students due to legal mandates and regulations. Confidentiality of information is always your best friend when dealing with special education students (SEdS) and special education in general. It is essential to know the federal, state, and local guidelines about special education and be aware of the laws to avoid any problems. As teachers, we have to research and be in the know about the current policies, rules, and regulations. The more you know, the less you can share due to confidentiality. Several mandates protect the rights of students with disabilities, and every individual should know them. Often these laws evolve. When you know these laws, you protect your students and, even more so, yourself. You make others aware that students with disabilities have the same rights as others.

In this chapter you will learn the meaning of special education; its history, or timeline; types of disabilities, accountabilities, laws; the age of transition; early intervention; least restrictive environment; and procedural safeguards. It is important to know this information so that we can be careful with our words when we converse with others and are informed. The laws are important in allowing us to understand why special education exists and what our roles are in ensuring we treat our students with disabilities with equality and respect.

What is Special Education?

US Department of Education (2017) has defined special education as: "specially designed instruction, at no cost to the parents, to meet the unique needs of a child with a disability, including—instruction conducted in the classroom, in the home, in hospitals and institutions, and other settings; and instruction in physical education" (p. 1).

Also, special education is a broad term used in the Individuals with Disabilities Act (IDEA) to describe specially designed instruction that meets the unique needs of students with disabilities (SWDs). These services are provided at home, school, classrooms, hospitals, public places, or institutions and are free of charge (Understanding Special Education, 2020).

Special Education Timeline

Preceden (2020) highlights the timeline of special education, or how and when it started. Special education began in the year 1817 and progressed and developed over the years. Being a SET requires awareness of the existence of how legislators created and changed laws and guidelines over time due to the evolution of special education services (SES) in the community.

- **American School for the Deaf**, April 15, 1817: The American School for the Deaf was founded in Hartford, Connecticut, and was the first school for SWDs anywhere in the Western Hemisphere (Preceden, 2020).
- **Perkins Institution for the Blind opens**, 1832: Founded in Boston, Massachusetts, this school was the first of its kind for people with mental conditions. Participants lived and learned in a fashion a boarding school (Preceden, 2020).
- **Law Mandating Compulsory Education**, 1840: Originated in Rhode Island, this law mandated a compulsory education for all children, which meant children were required by law

to receive education and governments had to provide such (Preceden, 2020).

- **Columbia Institution,** 1864: The US Congress allowed the Columbia Institution for the Deaf and Dumb and Blind authorized to grant college degrees. This institution was a worldwide pioneer for people with disabilities (Preceden, 2020).

- **Association of Instructors of the Blind**, 1870: "The School for the Deaf and the School for the Blind offered comprehensive educational programs for deaf, hard of hearing, and visually impaired students" (Preceden, 2020, para. 1).

- **Plessy versus Ferguson**, 1896: The Supreme Court upheld in Louisiana a separate car act. Plessy was arrested for riding in a white section on a train. It set the precedence of separate but equal (Preceden, 2020).

- **Beattie versus the Board of Education**, 1919: This case involved the expulsion of SWDs due to facial abnormalities and drooling. The students' mental capacities were excellent, but their physical conditions nauseated teachers and fellow students (Preceden, 2020).

- **Council for Exceptional Children (CEC)**, February 24, 1922: CEC is the first advocacy group for students with special needs. The primary objective is to ensure that children with special needs receive FAPE (Preceden, 2020).

- **The Bradly Home**, 1931: Established in East Providence, Rhode Island, this was the first psychiatric hospital for children in the United States (Preceden, 2020).

- **Cuyahoga Council for Retarded Citizens,** 1933: Also known as the Parental Advocacy Group, this body was composed of five mothers of children with mental retardation. These mothers came to Cuyahoga, Ohio, to protest their children's exclusion from public schools. This led to the establishment of a special class for the children, even though the parents sponsored it (Preceden, 2020).

- **Classification of Autism**, 1943: Dr. Leo Lanner of John Hopkins University introduced the classification of autism (Preceden, 2020).
- **National Association for Retarded Citizens (NARC)**, October 20, 1950: Twenty-three individual advocacy groups with the same beliefs formed the NARC group. The NARC had over two hundred thousand members at the time of the passing of the IDEA and the former helped with the litigation ensuring that all requirements of the judicial process were met (Preceden, 2020).
- **Brown versus the Board of Education**, May 17, 1954: A landmark court case that overturned Plessy versus Ferguson with the statement "Separate is not equal." This court case brought attention to black versus white students and SWDs versus regular education children which led the creation of several advocacy groups to inform the public of the need for special education programs (Timetoast, 2020).
- **Elementary and Secondary Education Act (ESEA)**, January 1, 1965: This act did not make it law to educate SWDs, but it gave grants to state schools and institutions that put into place programs to educate SWDs (Preceden, 2020).
- **Pennsylvania Association for Retarded Children versus Commonwealth of Pennsylvania**, October 8, 1971: This case sided with students with intellectual and learning needs in institutions run by the state. It "called for SWDs to be placed in a publicly funded school setting that met their individual educational needs, based on proper and thorough evaluation" (Timetoast, 2020, para. 1).
- **Mills versus the Board of Education of the District of Columbia**, December 17, 1971: The US District Court for the District of Columbia classified certain students as "exceptional"; this included those with mental and learning needs and behavioral issues. This ruling made it unlawful

for the DC Board of Education to deny these people access to publicly funded educational opportunities (Preceden, 2020).

- **First Center for Independent Living opens**, January 1, 1972: Ed Roberts created the center at UC Berkeley to "support the needs of SWDs so they could live independently and away from nursing homes and other institutions" (Preceden, 2020, para. 1).

- **Section 504**, September 26, 1973: Section 504 of the Rehabilitation Act provides protection from discrimination against students with disabilities (SWDs). It is the first law considered to give protection to SWDs. This law includes FAPE and LRE, in which SWDs that inhibit their learning are eligible (Preceden, 2020).

- **Education for All Handicapped Children Act**, 1975: This act assured that all SWDs were educated in public schools, which included free education, special education for children ages three through twenty-one, supplemental services, due process, zero rejection, and the LRE (Preceden, 2020).

- **Least Restrictive Environment (LRE)**, 1975: Students with IEP must also be in several regular education classes to ensure students have social experiences. In the LRE setting, paraprofessionals are needed. The law requires, to the maximum extent possible, SWDs will be educated together with students without disabilities (B. I. G. Solutions, 2017).

- **Board of Education of HHCD versus Rowley**, June 28, 1982: "Designed the Rowley Two-Part test in determining whether FAPE is being met according to a student IEP" (para. 1). It consists of "questions asking if the school fulfilled the procedures of IDEA and 'Is the IEP developed through the procedures of the act?' If these two questions are answered correctly, then FAPE and IDEA have been met" (Timetoast, 2020, para. 1).

- **Handicapped Children's Protection Act**, August 6, 1986: Ronald Regan signed the Handicapped Children's Protection Act, which allowed parents of SWDs more say in the development of their child's IEP.
- **Americans with Disabilities Act (ADA)**, July 26, 1990: The ADA was signed into law by President George W. Bush. The act promised that SWDs would have the same rights as others, either at school or at work. Also, it stated that SWDs could not be discriminated against in schools, the workplace, and even on public transportation (Preceden, 2020).
- **IDEA**, October 30, 1990: George W. Bush signed into law IDEA, which includes the six pillars "Free Appropriate Public Education (FAPE), Least Restrictive Environment (LRE), Individualized Education Plan (IEP), evaluation, parent/student participation, and all procedural safeguards for participants. This law also has four sections" (Preceden, 2020).
- **No Child Left Behind (NCLB) Act**, January 8, 2002: President George W. Bush signed this into law. It states that all students should be proficient in math and reading by 2014. Some states asked not to be part of this law. "Some schools have been caught falsifying scores, while others took it seriously and reported if they were not proficient" (Preceden, 2020, para. 1).
- **IDEA Reauthorized**, December 3, 2004: "The reauthorization of IDEA made many changes to the original. The changes include the IEP, due process, and student discipline" (Preceden, 2020, para. 1).

Every Student Succeeds Act (ESSA)

The US Department of Education recently put in place a new education law—ESSA. President Obama signed it on December 10, 2015. The bipartisan measure reauthorized the fifty-year-old ESEA, "the nation's national education law, and longstanding commitment to equal opportunity for all students. This law builds on key areas of progress in recent years, through the efforts of educators, communities, parents, and students across the country" (US Department of Education, n.d., p. 1). This new law represented good news for our country's schools.

The previous version of the law, the No Child Left Behind (NCLB) Act, was enacted in 2002. NCLB represented a significant step forward for our nation's children in many respects, particularly as it shined a light on where students were making progress and where they needed additional support, regardless of race, income, zip code, disability, home language, or background. The law was scheduled for revision in 2007, and over time the NCLB's prescriptive requirements became increasingly unworkable for schools and educators. Recognizing this fact, the Obama administration in 2010 joined a call from educators and families to create a better law that focused on the explicit goal of adequately preparing all students for success in college and careers.

cdschools.org

NCLB and Accountability

NCLB put in place measures that exposed achievement gaps among traditionally underserved students and their peers and spurred a meaningful national dialogue on education improvement. This focus on accountability has been critical in ensuring a quality education for all children yet also revealed challenges in the effective implementation of the goal.

Parents, educators, and elected officials across the country recognized that a strong, updated law was necessary to expand opportunity for all students; support schools, teachers, and principals; and strengthen our education system and economy.

In 2012 the Obama administration began granting flexibility to states regarding specific requirements of NCLB in exchange for rigorous and comprehensive state-developed plans designed to close achievement gaps, increase equity, improve the quality of instruction, and increase outcomes for all students.

Special Education Laws

All special education laws are covered by federal law, such as the IDEA. Rosen (2020) has stated that federal law lists out all that states must do to meet the needs of students with disabilities. However, IDEA allowed states to interpret the rules and their application.

States cannot contradict IDEA mandates. They can offer more protection to the students, but they cannot provide less for the students. IDEA stated that students who qualify in one of the thirteen disabilities might be eligible for SES. Rosen (2020) added that to be eligible, a student must have a disability that adversely affects their educational performance.

Free Appropriate Public Education (FAPE)

Each child is eligible for a free appropriate public education (FAPE). Students with SES must also receive the least restricted environment (LRE). There must be a continuum of placements available, from inclusion settings to self-contained settings. Rosen (2020) has explained that states must provide FAPE and must educate students with disabilities in the LRE setting but have a choice as to how to structure their schools and which educational programs to use as long as the students are provided service under FAPE and LRE. In most cases, the IEP team should provide the LRE to the student.

The Family Education Rights and Privacy Act (FERPA)

The US Department of Education (n.d.) defines FERPA as "a Federal law that protects the privacy of student education records. The law applies to all schools that receive funds under an applicable program of the U.S. Department of Education" (p. 1). FERPA deals with access to educational records, parental right to inspect and review records, amendment of documents, and destruction of records. Schools must notify parents and eligible students of their rights under such law. All information should remain confidential and can only be shared with the appropriate personnel and staff. Any personnel or staff needs to be trained in confidentiality as well.

Least Restrictive Environment (LRE)

According to SpecialEdNews (2020), LRE refers to a classroom placement of a student with disabilities in which the child can have the most freedom to be a child. This varies according to the needs of the student—minimal time in the classroom can be an LRE, whereas a student with moderate to severe disabilities can also be in an LRE setting. The LRE is also dependent on the student's evaluation or reevaluation results as prepared by the pupil appraisal or any evaluation committee that handles such evaluations. Also, the LRE can be determined during an IEP meeting by the IEP team.

Procedural Safeguards

According to Lucas and Walsh (2020), procedural safeguards are required by the IDEA, which is intended to protect the interest of families and children with special needs, as well as special education and early intervention systems. Procedural safeguards are the checks and balances of the system, not a piece separate from the system. Schools and parents can undergo evaluation, attend meetings, and dispute resolution. Typically, it takes about sixty days to process a child's evaluation to receive eligibility in special education. Some cases may take longer, depending on the circumstances of the evaluator or the people involved.

Early Intervention

Lots of skills develop between birth and age three, while some children meet developmental milestones more slowly than others, which can cause developmental delays (DDs). Morin (n.d.) stated that early intervention helps children with DDs catch up. Columbia University (2020) also noted that early intervention is "a set of SES designed to meet the needs of infants, toddlers, and preschoolers. A guarantee that your child with disability or DDs will receive appropriate services from infancy through their entire schooling career" (p. 1).

Age of Eligibility

Federal funding eligibility for states providing special education programs for students under IDEA must operate within the legal constraints of the law in defining age eligibility criteria. If a student between the ages of three and twenty-one meets the definition of "disabled" under the IDEA criteria, the student must be provided funding for IEPs support and resources in school communities (Bright Hub Education, 2020).

Age of Transition Services

Beginning at age sixteen (or before if appropriate), an annual IEP must include appropriate measurable postsecondary goals, transition services and courses of study, and a statement that the child has been informed of their rights transferring at the age of majority (Pacer.org, 2019). In the case of transition IEPs, the child must be invited, and his or her preferences must be considered. Representatives of agencies providing transition services must also be requested.

The rights of parents under IDEA are transferred to the SWDs at the age of majority (eighteen in most states) unless the child is determined to be incompetent. The school must notify both the child and the parent.

A student receiving an SES should have a transition services page in place by age sixteen. This form is to be completed no later than the first IEP to be in effect when the student turns sixteen years (or before, if determined appropriate by the IEP team) and updated annually. Here you are to interview the student about their dreams, desires, outcomes, and necessary actions that will then drive the development of the instructional goals and objectives.

Types of Disabilities

Under the IDEA, there are thirteen categories in which a student between the ages of three and twenty-one is eligible to receive the protections and services promised by this law (Special Education Guide, 2020). "To qualify for special education services, the IEP team must determine that a child has a disability in one of the 13 categories and must adversely affect their educational performance" (B. I. G. Solutions, 2017, p. 1). These are:

1. Autism
2. Deaf-blindness
3. Deafness
4. Emotional disturbance
5. Hearing impairment
6. Intellectual disability
7. Multiple disabilities
8. Orthopedic impairment
9. Other health impairments
10. Specific learning disability
11. Speech or language impairment
12. Traumatic brain injury
13. Visual impairment

CHAPTER 2: ADDRESSING NEEDS IN IEP CONFERENCES

If a child cannot learn in the way we teach…
we must teach in a way the child can learn.
—Dr. O. Ivar Lovaas

Overview

When I did my IEP for my first meeting with a parent, I was literally clueless about what to do. Yes, I had attended the orientation provided by the instructional specialist, but there was so much information conveyed in such a short period of time that it did not sink into my brain at that time. Plus, my knowledge of the individualized education plan (IEP) extended far beyond what I was learning during my special education classes. As I have said, I came from another country, and the information I learned was very limited. So in my first IEP meeting, I needed some guidance from an expert. I had to bring the thick handbook to my house to study it again, allowing the details to sink in for the second time. I could hardly believe that there were so many documents to prepare for just one IEP meeting, and these documents have to be completed beforehand, so when the meeting comes and the participants are gathered, the conference will run as smoothly as possible.

Little did I know that preparing an IEP meeting involved so many elements, from contacting parents to liaising with general education teachers, administration, and any other personnel that needs to be involved in the meeting. These people need to be notified at least fifteen days before the IEP. Not only that, but the information should also be included in the parent contact information to prove that you have communicated with the parents and others involved in the meeting. The start is always overwhelming. As a new SET, the tasks are so immense because you have to complete the steps for an upcoming IEP meeting at the same time you are serving as a support provider for your students in the classrooms. I have always heard from new SETs that they are tired in the first few months, and some even feel like quitting their jobs due to the many demands of paperwork and teaching at the same time, in addition to schools' almost-daily meetings.

Most SETs do not have adequate planning time, especially if there are two or more IEP meetings set for a given week. There are also amendment IEP meetings that need to be organized from time to time. Amendment IEPs can be done at any time when there's a need to change the child's IEP. The processes of conducting an annual review and an amendment of IEPs are very similar. If you need to write down the tasks involved in conducting an IEP meeting, you may do so. You will need it for the first few IEP meetings you will do. IEP meetings can be overwhelming as well. Treat it as a formal meeting in which the parents, the student, and other IEP participants discuss the child's progress or lack thereof in a year. All information remains confidential.

Being a SET is not easy. Your time is consumed by plenty of paperwork—inclusion logs, collaborations logs, IEP meetings, class data, amendments of IEPs, adding/deleting accommodations, adding health plans and other related services, failing grades, and transportation issues, to mention a few. However, it is only hard in the beginning. Once the teacher gets the routine in place—and with the right support from the administration, instructional specialist, and lead teachers—the next IEP meeting will be flawless.

I will address the need for an IEP conference because I believe that SETs must know how to conduct an IEP meeting and what preparations must be made before the meeting. It is good for a teacher to become familiar with the process so that the meeting will take place without mistakes. Every school has its own way of handling IEP conferences, so here I present general rules for successfully conducting an IEP conference.

One purpose of IDEA is to ensure all SWDs have available to them a FAPE that emphasizes special education and related services designed to meet each unique need by preparing the student for employment and independent living. This assurance is provided through an IEP.

In this chapter, you will learn about the meaning of an IEP, IEP team constitution, SET roles and responsibilities, how to develop an IEP, how to conduct an IEP, the components of writing an IEP, how to address IEP goals, see some sample ELA and Math SMART IEP goals, and learn about services, including school psychological services, and how to write progress reports.

What is an IEP?

The IEP is a written document that's developed for each public school child who is eligible for special education. The IEP is created through a team effort and reviewed and revised at least once a year (Baumel, 2019). Resnick (2009) further explains that:

> an IEP is a legal document. It is governed under IDEA, the Individual with Disabilities Education Act, which assures that services meet state and federal requirements. A school district is obligated to provide the services, supports, accommodations, and the number of minutes documented in the IEP. Progress is to be monitored consistently through data collection. If a child is not making gains on his/her goals, these goals need to be reevaluated and possibly revised. (p. 4)

IDEA is a federal law that requires certain information to be included in the IEP but does not specify how the IEP should look. Because states and local school systems may include additional information, forms differ from state to state and may vary between school systems within a country. There is no right or wrong way to conduct an IEP meeting. Just ensure that all the pertinent information is gathered and will be discussed during the conversation between the IEP team members.

IEP Team Members

Baumel (2014) has stated that the members of the IEP team include:

1. The parent(s), who can offer valuable insights and information about the student's strengths and support needs and ideas for enhancing the student's education

2. General education teacher(s), who can share information about classroom expectations and the child's performance

3. A SET that has training and experience in educating children with disabilities and in working with other educators to plan accommodations

4. Evaluation team member—an individual who can interpret the results of the child's evaluation and use findings to help plan an appropriate instructional program. Usually, it is the pupil appraisal who will be present during an IEP meeting.

5. Direct or related service provider—a representative of the school system who knows about special education services and has the authority to commit resources

6. The representative of any agency—an individual with knowledge of or particular expertise about the child who is invited by the parent and the school district

7. Representatives from transition services agencies, when such services are being discussed

8. The child, when appropriate, and whenever transition is discussed

9. Officially designated representative (ODR)—the principal or school administrator assigned as an ODR to the meeting

Special Education Teachers' Roles

Parents often feel overwhelmed when they attend an IEP meeting because so many people are present. The time goes by quickly, and you may feel rushed. Education jargon can be hard to understand, yet you are supposed to be a full participant in the meeting. Baumel (2014) has offered some ideas for parents that may help to reduce their anxiety, increase their participation, and facilitate the process as they interact with the IEP team members during the meeting:

1. Communicate regularly with school staff to have an idea of what the teachers may say at the meeting.

2. Prepare your thoughts before the meeting by writing down the essential points you want to make about your child. If you would like, ask to have your information included in your child's IEP.

3. Take someone with you to serve as your support system. If a spouse or family member cannot attend, ask a trusted friend to go with you. If you decide to bring a friend or advocate, you should inform the school so they are aware of whom you are bringing. Be prepared for them to question who the person is and why you have decided to include them in the meeting. The school should tell you if they have a specific policy on other attendees at the IEP meeting.

4. Ask questions if you do not understand the terms being used. If necessary, arrange to meet with individuals after the meeting to review their statements or reports.

5. Try to stay focused and positive. If anyone becomes frustrated or angry, ask to continue the meeting at another date. It is hard to develop an IEP when emotions have taken over the process.

6. Remember that you can sign to show you participated in the meeting, but you do not have to agree to the goals or services at the meeting.

In this way, SETs can assure to parents and the rest of the IEP team members that the meeting can be as productive and informative as possible.

Development of IEPs

SETs are an essential part of an IEP team. Arkansas State University (2016) stated that in addition to remaining compassionate and respectful toward special needs students and their families, SETs assist in the development of IEPs in the following ways:

- Bringing a comprehensive knowledge of learning challenges and disabilities

- Having the ability to suggest appropriate technologies or modifications to ensure a productive learning environment for children with different disabilities
- Possessing a complete understanding of legal and ethical parameters for providing education to special needs students
- Offering experience in delivering positive behavior modifications for a wide range of behavioral challenges
- Advocating for least restrictive learning environments, with an emphasis on special needs children learning alongside peers without disabilities whenever possible

Components of Writing IEPs

The IEP documents consist of different pages with different information. Familiarize yourself with each definition, and remember your student as you read and provide them information based on each data point, and prepare the student data that goes with each section as needed. Writing an IEP is crucial to the academic success of students with disabilities as it shapes their college and career readiness beyond coursework. Parts of the following description are adapted from the Louisiana Department of Education Special Education Reporting System (SER).

1. **Transition Page:** Each child receiving special education services should have a transition page in place by age sixteen. This form is to be completed no later than the first IEP to be in effect when the student turns sixteen years old (or younger, if determined appropriate by the IEP team) and updated annually. The dreams, desires, outcomes, and necessary actions will drive the development of the instructional goals and objectives. Also included on the transition page is the anticipated date of exit of the student in the school. Instruction or related services will also need to be part of the transition IEP, and in other situations, agencies are invited as well. It contains the school, student, family, and agency actions for linkages (these are advocates or communities who can support or hire students with disabilities).

2. **General student information**: This page contains the student's personal information, such as birth date, grade, state identification number, local identification number, date of the IEP, current grade and class, school the student last attended, name of the local education agency, names of IEP participants, and the school the student currently attends. You can also add what the student likes, whether the student has been retained, and when the student starts receiving services or whether the IEP is an initial, interim, annual, or an amendment IEP.

This also contains general information about the student—strengths, parent concerns, evaluation results (either school-based or district-wide assessments), academic/functional needs, statewide assessment results, progress or lack of progress, behavior, communication needs, including instruction in braille, assistive technology, and health services. Each state has a different IEP format, but IEPs tend to be similar across states. Other countries may require similar information.

There are three types of IEP: *interim, initial,* and *review.* The **interim IEP** is developed with students who have severe or low incidence impairments documented by a qualified professional concurrent with evaluation according to the pupil appraisal handbook. The interim IEP can also be developed for students who have been receiving services in another state concurrent with an assessment. Also, it is designed for students out of school, including students' ages five and above who are suspected of having a disability, and for previous special education students through the age of twenty-two who have left a public school without completing their public education by obtaining a state diploma.

The interim IEP may be used to provide special education services in the following situations temporarily: as part of the evaluation process, before the IEP is finalized, to aid in determining appropriate services for the student; when an eligible student has moved from one local education agency (LEA), and a copy of the current IEP is not available, either the LEA, AEA or parent believed that the current IEP is not appropriate; or additional information is needed before a final decision can be made regarding the specific special education and related services that are needed (Iowa IDEA Information, p. 1). Typically, placement occurs ten school days after entry.

The **initial IEP** is developed for a special education student who has met the criteria for one or more exceptionalities outlined in the pupil appraisal handbook and who has never received special education services except through an interim IEP. "An initial IEP (the first one) must be in place within the 30 days of the evaluation determining eligibility" (SpecialEducationGuide, 2020, p. 1). Initial IEPs need parent signatures, so parents must attend the meetings and sign the IEP documents. Without the parent signature, the IEP will not be in place and the student may not receive the services intended for the child.

The **review IEP** is reviewed and revised annually or more frequently to consider the appropriateness of the program, placement, and any related services needed by the student. Partners Resource Network (2020) stated that:

> The meeting brings the IEP team together to review the student's progress and program, and plan for the following year. As with other IEP meetings, the school district must provide parents with the advance written notice of the meeting and consider their availability when scheduling the meeting. (p. 1)

All three types of IEP require a prior written notice that the IEP participants should be present during the meeting. Though phone calls and emails are considered formal ways of communicating with parents, the written parental notice is important as this will be submitted together with the other IEP documents. You can document that you called or emailed parents in the contact logs as well.

3. **Instructional Page**: Instructional information such as present levels of academic performance, annual goals, and short-term objectives are provided for each subject area in which special education services are needed. The related services programs that will be delivered should also be addressed in these goals and objectives. Goals should not be changed unless an IEP meeting is held to reconvene. Necessary information, such as the student's academic/functional needs, strengths, weaknesses, progress monitoring, school or district assessments results, and learning styles, should also be included. It contains functional goals and short-term objectives. It also includes personnel responsible for implementing services to the student. For short-term objectives, write the date on which the student achieves the targeted goals.

4. **Accommodations** are changes in the way a student accesses learning without changing the actual standards by which the student is working toward their goals. It needs to be aligned with or matched to classroom instruction and testing and district or state tests. Students need to have opportunities to learn to use accommodations in classroom settings, and they also need to be able to take classroom tests using accommodations. "Testing conditions in the classroom should be as close as possible to those of the district or state testing situations to increase student's comfort level and allow for the best possible performance" (Kansas University, n.d., p. 1).

This page includes different types of accommodations—environment, instruction, materials, tests or quizzes, time, and assistive technology to be provided to the student with disabilities. Accommodations change how the student learns and the ways they demonstrate what they have learned. Special needs students are working on the same instructional objectives and concerns as other students. All staff servicing the students will also receive the student's individual accommodations, and this might include bus drivers as well.

5. **Program/Services** contains the LEA program, the type of statewide assessment the student will take, the accommodations the child will have for the state test, regular classes, activities with nondisabled peers, extended school year program, support needed for school personnel, special transportation. The IEP team can add comments or information required to clarify a student's instructional program.

6. **Placement** contains the student's special education instructional minutes, services, beginning date, duration, and the minutes required if in the regular, community, or special class. Also, it contains the placement and service determination checklist and the documentation of the education benefit for the placement if the student is not inside the regular class at least 80 percent of the day.

   Placement differs according to the age of the child. Placement might be in the regular classroom as an inclusion student, in a self-contained resource, a special education program, at home, or at a service provider location. Then a site determination is signed if it is noted that the site for the child is selected. Progress reports, age of majority, an alternative to regular diploma options, parent decision, supporting documentation, and parent and ODR signatures are also required.

   After each IEP meeting, either initial, interim, review, or amendment, always provide a copy to the parents and to the staff responsible for servicing the student. Use a dissemination page to document that these pages of the IEP have been disseminated to the appropriate staff.

How to Address IEP Goals

Every student with disabilities has a goal to achieve based on their weakness area. IEP goals can number more than one, and these are the goals on which the special education teacher works with the student over the IEP duration. At the end of every nine-week or grading period, the teacher will see whether the student is making progress satisfactorily or needs improvement on the set goals. Watson (2019) has stated that "Writing IEP goals correctly is vital to a SWD's success because they are legally entitled to an education plan specifically tailored to their cognitive and physical ability and needs. The IEP goals lay out the roadmap for providing such an education" (p. 1).

There are two main things a special education teacher can do to address IEP goals. First, ensure that the goals are aligned with the state standards or the standards your school district has set for students. The curriculum is attached to a grade-level standard set forth by the Department of Education. We know that a special education student is below functioning level as compared to their peers, so it is significant to set goals that are grade-level standards. We want our special education students to work toward the goals of normalcy. Second, ensure that your goals are SMART (specific, measurable, attainable, results-oriented, and time-bound). Each child's IEP should have SMART goals related to each weakness area. Watson (2019) has explained that SMART goals should be realistic and include a plan of action. Also, SMART IEP goals always consider the student's present levels of academic performance and include a brief description of how progress will be measured, as well as what constitutes successful completion of each goal.

Once the IEP team has agreed on a set of goals for the year, it is essential to monitor the student's progress toward meeting those goals. Since goals are written to cover an entire year, they are generally broken into benchmarks or short-terms. These might be quarterly periods where the teacher and staff can monitor how well the student is progressing toward the specific goal.

Sample SMART Reading IEP Goals

(Adapted and revised from A Day in Our Shoes with Lisa Lightner)

Sample reading goal 1: When presented with a text on the student's instructional level, he/she will be able to use context clues to determine the meaning of unfamiliar words in reading materials with 80% accuracy, as measured by written work samples, by the end of (IEP date).

Sample reading goal 2: When asked and probed, the student will be able to identify homonyms, synonyms, and antonyms and use these appropriately in sentences with 75% accuracy in four of five trials over an IEP year as measured by completed work samples.

Sample reading goal 3: After reading a passage and with teacher modeling, the student will be able to understand the passage's tone, character, point-of-view, and theme four out of five times with 80% accuracy over an IEP period as measured by student's work samples.

Sample reading goal 4: After reading a non-fiction story, the student will be able to explain the sequence of events either orally or in writing with 75% accuracy four of five trials over one IEP year as measured by student's work samples.

Sample reading goal 5: After reading a grade-level passage or text, the student will be able to recognize the difference between fact and opinion three out of five times with 75% accuracy over an IEP period as measured by student's weekly grades.

Mathematics SMART IEP Goals

(Adapted and revised from Virginia Department of Education, 2019)

Sample geometry goal 1: Given an assortment of three-dimensional (solid) concrete figures, the student will identify, describe, and sort these figures with 80% accuracy in eight out of ten trials over an IEP year as measured by the student's work samples.

Sample geometry goal 2: Given 10 problems involving the sum or difference of two whole numbers, each 9,999 or less, with or without regrouping, the student will solve with 80% accuracy using various computational methods over an IEP year as measured by the student's work samples.

Sample computation and estimation goal 1: Given 10 problems involving the sum or difference of two whole numbers, each 9,999 or less, with or without regrouping, the student will solve with 80% accuracy using various computational methods in three out of four trials over an IEP year as measured by the student's work samples.

Sample computation and estimation goal 2: Given a set of five single-step problems involving addition and subtraction of fractions and mixed numbers with like and unlike denominators, the student will solve them with at least 80% accuracy on three consecutive days by the end of the third grading period as measured by teacher's documentation logs.

Sample pattern, functions, and algebra goal 1: When shown the first four steps of a pattern, the student will extend the pattern three steps with 90% accuracy on three consecutive days by the end of the third grading period as measured by the student's progress monitoring.

Sample pattern, functions, and algebra goal 2: When shown the first four steps of a pattern, the student will extend the pattern three steps with 90% accuracy on three consecutive days by the end of the third grading period as measured by the student's progress monitoring.

Sample probability and statistics goal 1: Given experiments using spinners and colored tiles/cubes, the student will accurately record and use data to predict which of the two events are more likely to occur if the experiment is repeated in seven out of ten trials with 85% accuracy by an annual review of the IEP as measured by teacher's documentation records.

Sample probability and statistics goal 2: Using collected data, the student will be able to display and interpret data in a variety of graphs and tables with 75% accuracy in six out of 8 trials over an IEP year as measured by the student's work samples.

Services

Some special education students may already have services in place; some may start receiving services during the year depending on their needs as they go through academic, physical, behavioral, emotional, or social difficulties. This can be outlined during the IEP or at the time the teachers or parent suspects the student needs such services.

Services allow for a student with a disability to benefit from special education. All services go through a screening and have to be documented in an IEP team meeting. These services can include any of the following:

- Speech/language therapy and audiology
- Itinerant hearing and vision
- Physical and occupational therapy
- Therapeutic recreation
- Counseling
- Orientation and mobility training
- Assistive technology

The provision of health services is coordinated through the nursing department at the department of special education. In the educational system, services are provided only when it can be documented that the student needs or requires the services to benefit from their special education program.

When a student is determined to be at risk through the screening, an evaluation is conducted by an appropriate and qualified service provider. The service provider is charged with completing a comprehensive, disciplined-specific assessment in compliance with the Pupil Appraisal Handbook if it is in Louisiana or the handbook from which the school gets its information based on the state the school is located.

During the assessment process, the evaluator must apply the minimum eligibility criteria. If, after the evaluation process, the student meets the eligibility criteria and the evaluating service professional recommends the service, the IEP team must determine the need concerning educational goals and objectives.

One purpose of the IEP is to serve as a communication tool for all participating parties to ensure that they know what the student's strengths and weaknesses are, what will be provided, and what the anticipated outcomes may be. The primary role of the service provider during this process is to assist the committee in determining the need for service toward educational goals and objectives and to identify the most appropriate method of service provision. Service delivery provision might take place on a weekly, monthly, or once-a-semester basis.

For physical or occupational therapy, a referral or a prescription from a licensed physician is required. The IEP committee may agree with the service needed; however, provision is contingent upon the medical referral used by each state. When adding one of these services, fill out the appropriate forms and submit them to the appropriate personnel ahead of the scheduled IEP team meeting. Usually, about fifteen days' notification gives time for specific staff to adjust their schedules and provide information for the child in need of the service.

When a student receives certain related services, amend an IEP to address adding or changing the service. Send notifications to the IEP participants involved in the amendment. Address the change on the IEP as an IEP team. Then provide a copy of the IEP to all personnel responsible for serving the student, including the bus driver if the child is receiving special transportation and emergency plans. Their signatures attest to the fact that they have received the copy and will implement the services accordingly. For example, if adding health plan services to the student, notify all the IEP participants at least ten days before the scheduled meeting—participants might include one of the parents, a general education teacher, one of the school administrators, ODR, nurse, and other personnel the parents want to invite to the meeting. Then complete the IEP amendment procedure. Make sure that all participants sign and date the IEP if it is an amendment meeting and sign only if it is an initial, interim, or review IEP. If one of the IEP participants could not attend, have them fill out an excusal form. The IEP participants must attend and participate in the scheduled meeting. If the amendment can also be completed via phone conference because a parent or other participants cannot come to the school, the ODR must be present during the meeting as they are responsible for making the IEP official.

In such circumstances, an IEP is required—meaning that the parent of the child receiving services will need to fill out a waiver of full and effective notice. This means that there are not enough days to notify participants and the parent waives their rights in order to hold the IEP conference.

What Are School Psychological Services?

- Developing behavioral concerns
- Progress monitoring interventions
- Individual counseling
- Group counseling
- Social skills training
- Anger management and conflict management training
- Study skills training
- Substance abuse prevention and intervention
- Crisis prevention and intervention
- Parent skills training
- Evaluating intervention and service delivery outcomes
- Coordinating services with other community agencies
- Conducting functional behavioral assessments and analyses
- Consulting with teachers and families
- Conducting formal and informal assessments
- Interpreting assessment results

What Are School Social Worker Services?

- Individual counseling
- Group counseling
- Conducting assessments of student needs that are individualized and providing information that is directly useful for designing interventions that address behaviors of concern
- Incorporating assessments in developing and implementing intervention and evaluation plans that enhance a student's ability to benefit from educational experiences

The decision for the Pupil Appraisal Counseling Services will be determined at the student's IEP meeting, with the identified service provider in attendance.

Special Education Progress Reports

Special Education Progress Reports are completed every nine weeks or grading period. Aside from the regular progress report received, every SET should also have an individualized progress report based on their individual instructional goals. Reports on each student are based on the data on the school's required assessment and the progress or lack of progress toward each instructional goal or objective the student makes during the nine weeks or grading period. Also, add comments on the student's performance throughout the nine weeks. Each instructional goal and objective will have a separate report, and each related service personnel will also input their description of each child receiving such services. Ensure the dates entered and the dates sent follow the district's requirement to avoid issues afterward. As a special education teacher, you are responsible for sending copies of progress reports to parents through the student or certified mail, if needed.

The "I" in the IEP

I am the chief advocate for my child
I will know my and my child's rights in the process
I will research state and district education policies
I will bring support as required
I will defend and fight for my child
I will not back down over their needs
I will never surrender their right to FAPE
I will be prepared for possible questions
I will keep a professional tone
I will ensure that the plan is "Individualized"
And is not generic in nature
I will ensure the school remembers that this is
About a person, and not a process
(militaryautism.org)

How to Conduct an IEP Conference

An IEP is held annually. Every school district has a different timeline set up for doing annual review IEPs. Some school districts choose the student's birth month (Griend, 2019), while other school districts set a different date for annual review meetings. Griend (2019) has remarked that summer IEPs follow a similar pattern as some schools conduct annual reviews even when school is out, while other schools conduct summer IEPs in the spring months. When the IEP draft is completed and the notices have been sent, it is time for conferences. The responsibility for setting the stage for a successful IEP meeting rests with the special education teacher. How a meeting is conducted can significantly affect its outcome; therefore, teachers should be aware of proper techniques for attending an IEP conference.

The Understood Team (2020) has outlined an IEP meeting at a glance:

- The annual IEP meeting is the time to review, revise, and update a special education student IEP.
- Every element of the IEP should be covered during the meeting.
- Significantly, the IEP meeting focuses on the student as an individual.

Meetings are essential and an essential part of a student's education. Parents and teachers have to meet to discuss the progress or lack of progress of a student. Meetings are necessary to evaluate whether a student needs to be in a special program. The following information provides you with tips on how to make an IEP meeting productive and successful.

General Considerations

- Make sure all participants know when and where the conferences will be held. Send a reminder email, call or text message to IEP participants about the meeting, and call parents to remind them of the meeting.
- The setting for the IEP meeting should be physically comfortable and as free of distractions as possible. It can be done in one of the classrooms with no students in it. You can place a No Disturb Sign outside your door as well if it is within the same building with other classrooms in it.
- Do not hold the conferences in a classroom where parents are required to sit in small chairs or at uncomfortably low tables. Make parents feel comfortable.

- Make sure all materials are present and within easy reach. One suggestion is to have all forms placed in a file folder and have them prepared before the IEP meeting.
- Allow no interruptions—place phones in silent mode, and put a do not disturb sign on the door.
- Allocate sufficient time for the meeting so no one feels being hurried, but keep the meeting focused and on task. Allow every participant to offer input during the meeting.

Conducting the Meeting:
- When all participants have arrived, begin the conference by introducing all of the participants.
- Remind all that the IEP meeting will address the child's unique needs or characteristics as well as all the specially designed instruction, services, and accommodations these needs or characteristics necessitate.
- Ask the parents if they received the education rights booklet.
- Review the progress of last year's IEP goals and objectives. It should be printed out in the student's IEP folder and on the web-based IEP. Close out previous IEP goals by indicating achieved or revised.
- Begin discussing the current year's IEP and explain that this IEP is a draft and will not be considered "official" until the end of the meeting, once all information has been reviewed, discussed, and signed by the parent and the ODR, validated, and officially submitted to SER.
- Handwrite any additional information on the "draft" IEP. Do not use corrective fluid in any form. If a correction is to be made, a single line should be drawn through the error or information you wish to delete.
- Follow the IEP format in the order of the IEP pages. Read the IEP information in its entirety. Do not leave out any details of the IEP as all information is valuable to the participants.

- Ask about parent concerns and other concerns of the IEP participants, and write them on the IEP.

After the Meeting

- Provide a copy of the IEP document to the parents and the ODR to make the IEP official.
- Thank everyone for participating in and contributing to the meeting.

The Understood Team (2020) has shared vital takeaways for all IEP team members:

- The IEP team must consider your questions, insights, and observations.
- If a team member cannot attend, they can join remotely, or you can postpone the meeting.
- You can invite guests to support you or provide information about your child.

Submitting the IEP

- Once the parent has signed the IEP, add updates to the IEP to the web-based program in its entirety.
- The IEP must be made official within forty-eight hours of the IEP meeting.
- Attach the appropriate IEP forms to the IEP for submission.
- Follow the IEP checklist to see if all of the documents needed have been completed.
- The special education personnel with the authority to certify the IEP as "official" will submit the IEP via the web-based program.
- An official copy will be submitted to the records department according to the submission dates listed on the IEP calendar or timeline established by the compliance department.

Griend (2019) has suggested things that a special education teacher should *not do*:

- Hold a conference with just you and a parent.
- Use the conference as a means of informing parents of daily happenings or discussing other students in the class or building.
- Share specific personal information—medical or social. Keep information about yourself general.
- Hold a conference with an attorney if the SBCSC attorney is not present. Should parents enter with an attorney, the special education office should be informed immediately, and the meeting will be rescheduled.
- Hold a conference regarding the BEST placement without preapproval from SES.
- Put a child on a reduced schedule or decide they should be homebound without a support team member present or consulted before the conference.
- Request testing without a school psychologist present or consulted before the conference.

Site Determination

Although the IEP team member must participate in the placement decisions of the student, the Local Education Agency or LEA has the obligation to determine the school site in keeping the team's decision. The personnel assigned to do the IEP shall be responsible for notifying the IEP participants. The IEP team must participate in decisions made about the placement; however, the LEA has the right to select the school site based on the committee's decisions. This form must be forwarded to the parents within ten calendar days. In most cases, the site determination section is filled out during the IEP meeting. A copy of this form should also be placed inside the student's IEP folder.

Conducting Virtual IEP Meetings

In some cases, IEP meetings cannot be held at the school. When the pandemic struck in the year 2020, most IEP meetings were conducted via a web-based online platform or phone calls. Who would have thought that this once-minor way of communicating with parents would become the most important way to conduct an IEP? Based on my observations, some IEP meetings held online and via phone are more successful than face-to-face meetings. Most parents can attend with just one call from the teacher. The pandemic has hit us hard in terms of handling IEP meetings, but we quickly figured out how to conduct them effortlessly and successfully with the IEP team present during the meeting.

An alternative platform should be in place. Nieves (2020) has stated that "many districts have turned to use Google Meet, Microsoft Teams, or other conferencing tools—with the consent of families to maintain the IEP timeline" (p. 1). Nieves (2020) further suggests eight tips for conducting virtual IEP meetings:

1. **Use the school's platform**: The school has preferences for an online platform to use for virtual meetings. Use it, and inform the participants of the platform so they can download the online conference. The online platform that is commonly used is Zoom meetings.

2. **Consider web platform alternatives**: If the school platform is not available or accessible, consider another type of platform—phone conference, Google Hangouts, Google Meets, and other web platform services. Sometimes, a combination can be used, with some participants in a Zoom meeting and others on a phone call. Just ensure that all hear the reading of the IEP information on the student.

3. **Synchronize district calendars**: Ensure that the schedule you set for the IEP meeting follows the district calendar to avoid out-of-time-line IEP conferences. One suggestion is to ensure all IEP participants and related services are provided with a parental notification of the IEP meeting ahead of time. Our school uses Google Docs that are shared with all personnel servicing the students. Also, the IEP meetings are synced with the email calendar so that we will be notified of the upcoming meetings.

4. **Have an agenda prepared**: To ensure a smooth transition to the IEP, have a list prepared, and inform the participants

who will speak that they should avoid choral responses or sharing of information. When someone speaks, the other participants should listen.

5. **Enable the confidentiality feature in emails** to ensure that the email messages reach the right person and the information remains confidential. Before sending an email notification to the parent, ensure the email address listed on the school's record is correct.

6. **Encourage student participation**: Sometimes students that are part of the IEP meeting can participate, ensuring that the student will have the opportunity to speak during the conference. The student can speak most clearly about the expectations outlined in the IEP. Parents need to be asked for permission, though, if the child is below eligibility age.

7. **Muting and unmuting**: Ensure that the sound is muted and unmuted appropriately to avoid background noises that will distract from the meeting. Inform each participant that they should unmute themselves if they want to speak, or the host can unmute any participant who wants to say something at the meeting.

8. **Do not forget parental input outside of IEP meetings**: Ensure that the parent shares their concerns, issues, or clarifications on the information shared during the meeting. The parent has a valuable contribution to make to the IEP concerning their child.

IEP Amendments

An amendment occurs when an IEP conference needs to reconvene after the IEP has been made official and sent to the web-based program. Resnick (2009) has stated that "although IEPs are written for one year, a parent does not have to wait for the Annual Review meeting to share their concerns. IEP Review meetings can be called at any time, and changes can be accomplished through IEP revisions" (p. 4). The following events require IEP amendments:

- Request for reevaluation
- Add health plan services
- Change instructional goals and objectives
- Reviewing behavioral concerns
- Increase/decrease in-service time
- Parent concerns
- Failing grades
- Change/delete accommodations
- Change in the program (alternate assessment, pre-GED skills options)
- Service delivery such as direct to consult, tracking, dismissal, and other types of delivery (e.g., student whose primary exceptionality is speech or language impairment, which will require a reevaluation for dismissal)
- Other reasons as determined by the IEP team

Parents must be notified via parental notification at least ten days before the IEP meeting. In some cases, parents must be provided with a waiver of full and effective notice of the reason for the conference. A full reevaluation is not required to address additional services or special services when a student has already been identified as exceptional due to a disabling condition.

Things to Remember during an Amendment IEP Meeting

Though the process of an amendment IEP is similar to that of an initial, review, or interim IEP, there are slight differences between these meetings. Amendment IEP meetings is not as time consuming as a regular review IEP. Based on experience and depending on the reason of the IEP, it can last less than thirty minutes. I have handled several amendment IEP meetings and there are things to remember during an amendment IEP meeting. IEP can be amended more than once when there is certain concerns or issues of the special education student that needs to be addressed.

Once the IEP teacher finds out that a child's IEP needs to be amended, the following are the steps to amend an IEP:

- The IEP teacher must call the parent notifying the reason for amending the IEP.
- Send parent notifications of the schedule amendment IEP meeting either via student or parent's email address.
- Send at least three parent notices and write this information on the parent contact log.
- Also, send this parent letter to the IEP team who will need to attend the meeting. If any of the IEP team member is unable to attend, let them fill out an excusal form on their absence.
- The original annual review date must be circled and indicate the new date of the amendment.
- During the meeting, the IEP holder will explain the reason for amendment.
- IEP participants need to indicate their presence either via phone, via online platform, or via in-person. They need to sign the document. If it is their first time attending the amendment IEP meeting, he/she needs to sign his/her full name and indicate the date of the meeting.
- If the IEP participant is already in the previous IEP meeting, let them put their initials and date of the amendment IEP.
- Ensure that the reason for amending the IEP is approved by the IEP team.
- Indicate parent's concerns on the IEP.
- Parents shall be given a copy of the amended IEP.
- The writings on the hardcopy of the IEP must match on the website where the IEP needs to be typed.
- A validation page needs to be printed. If all of the categories are checked, it means the IEP is ready to be submitted to the ODR.

IEP Folder Organization

IEP documents need to be placed in a pocket folder. Arrange only the current data in the appropriate pocket of the IEP folder. The old data must be placed in an old file using a manila folder in chronological order and must be attached to the IEP folder. Documentation must be kept on the IEP objectives. When a SETs transport the IEP folder to another school, it should remain intact. Ensure that all the supplementary documentation, such as collaboration logs, inclusion logs, progress monitoring results, and other pertinent assessment results, are placed in a supplemental folder and go with the IEP folder when transported to another school. The longer the student receives special education services, the thicker the supporting document stack; it should be included in the main IEP folder whenever the student moves to another school within the district. It is recommended to organize the IEP folder at least two times a semester. Sometimes, there is a local monitoring for folder check. Other times, there is a state-level monitoring. The folder check is done at random. It is better to make sure that all IEP folders are organized and files are up to date and in place.

CHAPTER 3: TYPES OF SPECIAL EDUCATION CLASSROOMS AND INCLUSIVE INSTRUCTION

Inclusion is not simply about physical proximity. It is about intentional planning for the success of all students.

Learning Knows No Bounds

Campverdesschools.org

When you accept the job as a special education teacher, the school administrator may assign you to a different type of classroom instruction. There are two major things you need to be an expert on in order to serve students with disabilities. First is the paperwork. The second is servicing your assigned students during the times you are not having an IEP meeting. It is not about meetings all day, five days a week.

You need to go to the classroom and provide support to your students based on the instructional goals and any other support the regular education teacher might ask you to provide in the classroom. You can also pull out your students at least once a week for additional instructional support.

The more years I put into my service, the more I learned about special education. Instructional time also varies according to how you support students. Some students may need more than thirty minutes. Some students may need less than thirty minutes. I was first appointed to be an inclusion teacher when I got the job as a special education teacher, but I learned the other types of classroom instruction as I visited the other special education classrooms. Whether you are an inclusion, resource, or self-contained teacher, you have to provide services to special education students to succeed. According to Special Education Resource, special education applies to

> Children with special needs who are attending a regular school, and assists children with a variety of disabilities. How special education is handled, however, changes from school to school? Some schools have still not caught up with the concept of special education; everyone is included in the general school population and given the same opportunities across the board, regardless of limitations, but supportive services are provided to help with individual accommodations. (pp. 2–3)

As special education teachers, we are equipped with the knowledge, expertise, respect, and compassion to support our students no matter which placement they are in. You should also know how to be flexible in the support you provide. Some students are easy to teach, while some students can be a challenge. Everyday experience can be different. Don't take students' mean words personally. Learn how to show compassion and care, and the students you serve will reciprocate the kindness shown in many other ways. Some teachers can be a challenge too. Teachers are territorial, and when you know you go to their classroom, you have to learn how to set boundaries without insulting them.

Regular education teachers have many misconceptions about having a special education teacher in their classrooms; you have to learn how to be flexible and professional at all times.

Remember the end goal: to serve the student with all inclusivity regardless of the classroom setup they are placed in. Also, remember that you and the general education teachers are there to provide support to the students. That is why it is important to collaborate with the regular education teachers so that they will be informed about the students you are servicing. Collaboration is key to achieving the successful support of students with disabilities in the regular education classroom.

Successful Inclusive Classrooms

As special education teachers, we ensure that students are active learners. Give students chances to explain their thoughts and express what they want to say. Most of the time, quiet students have something to say if given opportunities to share and speak in class. Doing this provides each child with confidence in themselves. Students should be encouraged to make choices. Giving choices allows flexibility for students to do certain things in the classroom. Create menus for students to choose from at a particular time at school. They will thus have the opportunity to do what they are interested in (but ensure that teachers are supervising students' work).

Parental involvement is crucial in a student's learning. Always communicate with parents. If you can do it daily, do it. Parents want to hear teachers calling them about what their children are doing at school. When calling parents, always start with the good news, followed by some bad news. Parents appreciate teachers who show they care about their children.

Give them opportunities to learn at their own pace. Special education students do not function the same way or learn the same way; give them time to learn. Accommodations and alternative assessment strategies are in place to meet their unique needs. IEP goals should be on grade level and meet grade-level standards.

Setting the Tone

Cox (2020) has stated that "one aspect of a teacher's job is to create a positive learning environment for their students, a place where students are not judged and feel comfortable learning" (p. 1). These are ways to set the tone for a fruitful year:

- **Build relationships**: As a teacher, you need to get to know your students on the first day you meet them. Lay down expectations for students to follow. Think of yourself as lucky to have these students. Make them feel welcome and appreciated. Show them that you are hopeful and positive about the class you have. Express that you hope everyone can do their best. Building relationships is key to a fruitful and successful year.

- **Celebrate diversity by creating a prejudice-free zone in the classroom**: Everyone is unique and has their own characteristics, so tell students to leave behind any stereotypes about other students. Explain that everyone in the classroom needs to be accepted and have a sense of belongingness. All should show respect to and acknowledgment of anyone else in the room. Show some videos or read articles that include a diversified population so that students will understand.

- **Educate yourself**: Know the current events around your school and community. Attend professional development that is offered at your school district. The knowledge gained from these workshops will greatly impact students' learning. Furthermore, learn to share information.

- **Have a positive attitude**: Amid all the things happening in a child's life, model a positive attitude in life. Create a positive atmosphere so students feel the presence of positivity in the classroom. Display positive quotes and sayings on the wall of the classroom for students to read. Create materials and activities that show positive messages, and students will adapt to the conveyed information. Be consistent, and you will see good results.

Types of Special Education Classrooms

Some schools rely on partial inclusion of children with special needs to serve this sector of the student body best, putting them in the company of other children while doing certain activities or subjects. The following are types of special education classrooms and instruction:

- **Mild-to-moderate students**: These students are typically in the general education classroom. Arkansas State University (2020) has explained that students with this kind of disability range from those with specific learning disabilities who struggle in math or reading to those with a speech-language impairment who may struggle with pronunciation. These students usually function within the regular education classroom with accommodations for inclusion and paraprofessional support. Even a student with a physical impairment such as hearing or health impairment can be considered mild. A student with a hearing impairment may just need a hearing device to hear in the classroom but may not need other accommodations to succeed. Usually, regular education teachers will have these types of students.

- **Moderate-to-Severe**: Students with "more severe disabilities are in special programs within the school with disabilities range from severe physical limitations, emotional disturbances, or extreme developmental delays. They stay in one room for the majority of the day, except for enrichments classes and lunch" (Arkansas State University, 2019, p. 2).

- **Autism**: This can also be called autism spectrum disorder (ASD) and "refers to a broad range of conditions characterized by challenges with social skills, repetitive behaviors, speech, and nonverbal communication. According to the Centers for Disease Control, Autism affects an estimated 1 in 54 children in the United States today" (Autism Speaks,

2020, p. 1). These children typically stay in one room for the majority of the school day and change rooms for enrichment or elective classes. Depending on the district, this class will typically have one autism teacher and two or more paraprofessionals in the classroom.

- **Inclusion**: This is also called "mainstreaming" and refers to students being educated with nondisabled peers for most of their school day. A special education teacher "collaborates with a general education teacher to provide services for students" (Special Education Degrees, 2013, p. 2). The general education teacher is responsible for teaching all children—with or without IEP. The special education teacher collaborates with the regular education teacher on strategies and other academic concerns. These students will follow the daily regular education class schedule, including lunch, recess, and enrichment. Each state in the country has specific standards in terms of inclusion support time, but typically the special education teacher serves students with disabilities in the inclusion setting for at least thirty to sixty minutes per core subject area, with pullout time as needed. Time varies according to the student's needs.

- **Self-contained:** These are classrooms specifically designated for SWDs "with more serious disabilities who is unable to participate in general education programs at all. These disabilities include Autism, emotional disturbances, severe intellectual disabilities, multiple handicaps, and children with serious or fragile medical conditions" (Webster, 2019, p. 1). Individual needs are supported in resource rooms as defined by the student's IEP. In this setting, the students remain in the self-contained classroom for reading, ELA, math, science, and social studies and will only go out for enrichment or elective classes.

- **Resource**: "A separate setting, either a classroom or a smaller designated room, where a special education program can be delivered individually or in a small group" (Watson, 2019, p. 1).

Teachers in the resource room play a challenging role as they need to design all instruction to meet the specific needs of the students they serve in order to maximize their learning potential. The resource room teachers work closely with the child's regular classroom teacher and the parents to ensure the support is indeed helping the student reach their full potential.

The teacher follows the IEP and takes part in the IEP review meetings. They also work very closely with other professionals and paraprofessionals to support the specific student. Usually, the resource room teacher works with a small group of students, helping one-on-one when possible, even though there are frequent occasions when the special education teacher follows one or multiple students in their classes and assists them directly there.

Resource students can only go out for certain core subjects, depending on the IEP team's decisions. Most students go to a resource setting if they need more restrictive instruction in either science or social studies. Some students only go for ELA, reading, or math (or some combination thereof).

• **Co-teaching**: A setup "in which a special education teacher and a general education teacher share the responsibility of providing instruction and assessments to students, which encompass both students with and without disabilities" (Schwartz, 2018, p. 2). When done well, this should enable students with disabilities to receive the general education curriculum and any exceptional services that they need in the same setting. It is more of a professional marriage because it requires excellent collaboration among teachers—from planning the lesson to strategies to use, classroom management, and how they run the classroom. The special education teacher stays in the regular education classroom most of the time and goes to the same planning and professional learning community meetings.

Both teachers should make contact with parents at the beginning of the year and must maintain regular parent contact throughout the year. Always collaborate for consistency of establishing procedures in the classroom—any addition or change made to the classroom in terms of instruction, discipline, or strategies. Both teachers must participate during parent conferences for students with disabilities.

Co-Teaching Approaches

Depending on the school district you are working in, you might be assigned to be the other teacher in the classroom, a term we call co-teaching. Cook (2004) has stated that

> Co-teachers often report that one of the most noticeable advantages of sharing a classroom is the sense of support it fosters. Co-teachers report that when they have a spectacular lesson, someone is there to share it, and when they have a particularly challenging day, someone knows just how difficult it was. (p. 7)

Cook further explains that co-teaching, when deliberately done, yields effective results.

1. **One teaches, one observes**: This is also called "one leads, one supports." When one teacher teaches and the other observes during co-teaching, the teachers should decide in advance what types of information are to be gathered during the observation and should agree on a system for collecting the data. Afterward teachers should analyze the information together. That is, observation should be a deliberate part of the lesson, not just teachers' incidental checks of student activity.

2. **One teaches, one drifts**: One teacher has more responsibility in the classroom, and the other teacher goes around the classroom and provides support to the students who need help.

3. **Parallel teaching**: In parallel teaching, co-teachers are teaching the same information, but they divide the class group and conduct the lesson simultaneously.

4. **Station teaching**: In this scenario, teachers divide content and students. Students rotate from one teacher to another and also to an independent station so that each teacher repeats instruction three times and each student accesses both teachers and the independent station. If appropriate, the third station could be set up to require that students work in pairs instead of independently. One teacher is teaching in each rotation. Rotation time differs depending on the class schedule.

5. **Alternative teaching**: The large group completes the planned lesson while the small group either completes an alternative lesson or the same lesson taught at a different level or for a different purpose. This arrangement might take an entire class period, or it might be used for just a few minutes at the beginning or end of a lesson.

6. **Team teaching**: Both teachers are delivering the same instruction at the same time. This implies that each speaks freely during large-group instruction and moves among all the students in the class. Teaching becomes a conversation, not turn-taking. Share some input with the class and come to a consensus about the topics to share with the students.

Roles of Special Education and General Education Teachers in Grading

General education teachers should be curriculum experts. It is their responsibility to keep an eye on all of the students in the classroom with the goal of mastering the curriculum. They work with special education students to make sure accommodations are implemented. And they can grade all students, not just the regular education students.

Special education teachers are strategy experts. They are the ones with expertise regarding how best to teach the students with or without an IEP. You focus on the IEP goals and inform the general education teacher of these goals and make sure they are making accommodations mandated by the IEP. You are responsible for every child in the class. You can take part in grading papers and can make recommendations and comments on the regular education students' needs. Grading responsibilities can be worked out between co-teachers.

Collaboration Strategies

- Assist all students.
- The special education teacher is not just a guest in the general education classroom. They need to provide accommodations for the student in the class.
- When walking into a co-teaching setting, the general education teacher and the special education teacher should work as a team. Not I, but we!
- They should collaborate and plan as often as possible.
- The ideal arrangement is 30 percent special education students per class maximum.
- Both teachers should look for different strategies to help all students, with or without IEPs.
- Both should know the students they serve.
- Know how to celebrate diversity.
- Both should participate in grade-level meetings and professional development meetings
- Work as a team at all times!
- Regularly communicate and reflect on the teaching.
- Review and discuss accommodations and IEP goals frequently.

- Use collaboration logs.
- Determine the best instructional methods / learning styles—visual, auditory, kinesthetic, and tactile—to fulfill individual needs

CHAPTER 4: WHY DIFFERENTIATION IN INSTRUCTION?

*Differentiation is simply a teacher attending to the learning needs
of a particular student or small groups of students, rather than
teaching a class as though all individuals in it were basically alike.*
—Carol Tomlinson

"If you desire to make a difference in the world,
you must be different from the world" (Elaine S. Dalton)

Adams and Pierce (2004) have stated that "the movement toward in-clusion has impacted classrooms by requiring teachers to respond to a broader range of academic needs" (p. 1). The authors added that "essential elements for successful differentiation include specific class-room management techniques addressing the special needs of a differ-entiated classroom, planned use of anchoring activities, and flexible use of time, space, and student groups" (p. 1). Furthermore, Bajrami (2013) has stated that

> differentiation puts the focus on learners, and it is a learn-er-centered approach that is aimed to help students suc-ceed regardless of the differences. In order to reach every student in the classroom, the teacher should always have students' diversity in mind, starting from the planning stage to designing activities to be used in the classroom and the teaching process and their assessment. (p. 1)

When Carol Tomlinson was interviewed at Curry School of Education and Human Development in 2017, she defined differen-tiation as "an instructional approach to help teachers teach with in-dividuals as well as content in mind. Differentiation means trying to make sure that teaching and learning work for the full range of stu-dents, which really should be our goal as teachers" (p. 1). Teachers have to learn how to differentiate to meet individual needs. Students have different ability and functional level and with these, teachers need to analyze students' data to provide the appropriate differentiation activ-ities. Tomlinson (2017) added that "if we take on the responsibility of teaching, we accept the responsibility of making sure that every kid learns as well as he or she possibly can" (p. 2). Providing differentiation while considering the student's learning style makes the classroom ex-perience meaningful and successful. Teachers have to consider provid-ing differentiating activities in teaching a core concept or skills to stu-dents. If teachers differentiate lessons, students become confident and comfortable to access the resource and be able to do their tasks. "By understanding what kind of learner your students have, you can now gain a better perspective on how to implement these learning styles into your lesson plans and study techniques" (Teach.com, 2020, p. 2). The more teachers use differentiating activities, the more students gain an understanding of the lesson at their own pace without decreasing the standards of learning. Students learn with the same grade level expectations as others except that the activities they work on are on their performance level.

Data supports the claim that differentiation in instruction is essential. Pangatungan (2018) has stated that "despite the US government's effort to boost the education system for students in America, millions of students continue to struggle in academics most especially in reading" (p. 14). In this way, the school has to do something to help these children learn and become successful in learning. Teachers have to find ways to differentiate lessons in a way that students grasp the activities in order to lessen the learning gaps. Robb (2020) has stated that, in 2003, "The US Department of Education reported that more than 8 million students in grades 4 through 12 are struggling readers" (p. 1). In addition, Huebner (2010) "confirms that differentiated instruction can enable students with a wide range of abilities—from gifted students to those with mild or even severe disabilities—to receive an appropriate education in inclusive classrooms" (as cited in Lawrence-Brown, 2004, p. 2). Teachers need to see to it that children are provided with what they need in order to learn effectively. For example, students can be given learning styles questionnaire to see to it that each kid in the classroom is catered to meet his or her academic needs. The results of the learning styles questions can be used to analyze and group students who have fall on the same category of learning. Robb (2020) has reported that "a full 70 percent of U.S. middle and high school students require differentiated instruction, which is instruction targeted to their strengths and weaknesses" (as cited in Biancarosa and Snow, 2004, p. 2). Identifying students' strengths and weaknesses help teachers group students according to their ability. The weaknesses can be lessened because of the teachers' acquiring the appropriate learning styles each student might have. Teachers can plan effectively differentiating lessons now that there is data to look into.

Relatedly, Adams and Pierce (2004) have stated that "in a differentiated classroom, the management plan must include rules for working in a variety of configurations. Teachers can only work with one group or individual at a time" (p. 2). Teachers need to understand that differentiating lessons is one of the instructional strategies to use to improve students' academic performance. To differentiate means to be able to see the need and level of support to students and not as a form of last resort to hep students improve their skills. And Pangatungan (2018) has further observed, "educators and parents needed to teach students about the determined practice and helped them adopt the necessary mechanisms to reach just beyond their current grasp" (p. 20). All personnel involved in improving student's academic performance has to work together to be able to fully support and meet the individual needs of students through differentiating activities.

Brulles and Brown (2018) argue that "many students learn and think differently from their peers. They need to understand, accept, and use their learning differences as assets when they are grouped. Consistent and appropriate academic challenge need to be provided to become comfortable with themselves and others" (p. 23). Huebner (2010) has observed that teachers usually differentiate instruction by adjusting one or more of the following: "the content (what students learn); the process (how students learn); or the product (how students demonstrate their mastery of the knowledge or skills)" (as cited in Tomlinson and Strickland, 2005, p. 2). Also, with an eye toward meeting the differing needs of students, Best (2020) has offered tips for teachers to differentiate their instruction: "content: the actual subject matter of their teaching; instruction: their teaching strategies and methods; product: the result that students produce; and environment: space where learning occurs" (p. 1).

Though most differentiation is geared toward reading, math differentiation can follow the same pattern for differentiating lessons so that students are successful in the classroom. Rogers (2017) has stated that

Differentiating math instruction is an important skill to have in order to meet the needs of the different learners in a classroom. Math objectives can be differentiated based on process, content, or product. The process is how the students learn information, content is what the students learn, and the product is how the students demonstrate their learning. When teachers can successfully execute one or more ways to differentiate, they can engage students in more meaningful learning. (p. 1)

A special education teacher's task is to differentiate lessons because students learn at different times, paces, and places. There are many ways to differentiate your class—*learning styles, tiering, metacognition, questioning, grouping, materials, and resources.*

Differentiation through Learning Styles

Children—and even adults—learn at different paces and have set preferences when it comes to learning. "The term learning styles is widely used to describe how learners gather, sift through, interpret, organize, come to conclusions about, and "store" information for further use" (Chick, 2020, p. 1). Furthermore, "When the student's needs are met, they are engaged in their learning. It not, they resort to disruptive behavior. Understanding their learning styles as well as their intelligence, teachers can differentiate the curriculum to students" (Bright Hub Education, 2020, p. 2). For example, if a differentiated class is assigned a science activity, some children might write a paper, while others might create a poster or PowerPoint presentation, and others might conceive of a skit or cartoon.

Smith (2018) has identified four different learning styles: visual, auditory, reading and writing, and kinesthetic:

- **Visual learning style**: Students who learn best through visual aids have a visual learning style. Visual aids include facial expressions and gesticulations of teachers, pictures, texts with illustrations, DVDs, and more. Visual learners think and learn in pictures.

- **Auditory learning style**: Some students prefer to learn by hearing what they want to learn. Theirs is the auditory learning style. In order to learn, such students prefer listening to discussions, talking matters over, reading out of texts, or making use of e-courses containing audio recordings.
- **Reading and writing learning style**: If a student learns best by reading texts or writing down notes based on what they read, see, or hear, then they are considered a reading and writing (R & W) learner. R & W learners need writing materials to take down points they think are relevant based on what they read, hear, or see.
- **Kinesthetic learning style**: Kinesthetic learners prefer to learn by moving and doing. They prefer interactive learning, learning through practical challenges and hands-on experience, and taking in information as they move from one place to another. Kinesthetic learners, therefore, are not comfortable sitting in one place for long.

Grand Canyon University (2020) has explained ways to support students with different learning styles:

- **Supporting visual learners**: Some of the more traditional styles of teaching, such as whiteboards or projecting information onto a screen, support visual learners. Assignments might ask learners to make pictures or diagrams. Also, providing class notes or handouts that students can follow along with is a great way to integrate visual learning into your curriculum. Visual learners may have a tough time with lectures and need more time to process information that they hear auditorily.
- **Supporting auditory learners**: Including significant time for discussion can support the auditory learners in your classroom. They want to hear what others have to say and share their ideas in order to learn and process information. When you are giving a lecture, ask auditory learners to repeat what they have learned back to you. Call-and-response

or question-and-answer processes can also benefit auditory learners. Furthermore, auditory learners appreciate watching videos about a topic and listening to audiobooks or recordings.

- **Supporting reading and writing learners**: Most of the traditional educational system caters to this type of learner. The reading and writing learner learns by researching, reading books, and writing. They will usually be content to write an essay or create a written project. While these students may not be as vocal as auditory learners, they can express themselves well with the written word. Try to give reading and writing learners time to write their answers and work through their thoughts on paper.
- **Supporting kinesthetic learners**: Since kinesthetic learners learn through movement, teachers may ask them to act out scenes from a book or use movement in other ways during the learning process. For example, a kinesthetic learner can benefit by walking in place or pacing in a small area while trying to memorize facts. Additionally, when learning can be associated with movement of some kind, such as teaching vocabulary using the total physical response method, kinesthetic learners may retain that information more readily. The kinesthetic learner who connects with something physically can use that information to understand more abstract and theoretical concepts.

The image below shows additional learning styles, beyond the four basic learning styles previously mentioned. What is your learning style?

Learning Styles

Each learning style has its advantages and disadvantages, but depending on the nature of the student, they can benefit from a combination of more than one learning style depending upon the situation or place of learning. Malvik (2020) has stated that

> Understanding the different learning styles does not end in the classroom. By equipping students with tools in their early years, teachers are equipping them for their futures. Pinpointing how a child learns best can dramatically affect their ability to connect with the topics you are teaching, as well as how they participate with the rest of the class. (p. 4)

Lam (2017) has further stated that with large classrooms, it is not always easy to personalize lessons, but using a mixed learning approach throughout coursework can help you cater to each type of learning style. You may decide to focus on a particular learning type in each lesson or incorporate multiple strategies within each lesson. The most important element is first recognizing the differences in student learning—the rest will flow from there.

Differentiation through Tiering

The other way to differentiate is through **tiering**: Educators need to design and deliver instruction that meets the individual needs of students in the classroom (Tiered Instruction: Definition & Method, 2017).

This is to say, "tiering is an instructional practice that allows the students the opportunity to journey toward grade-level standards. Tiered assignments are parallel tasks provided to small groups of students based on their similar levels of readiness to complete them" (EL Education, 2020, p. 1). When you create tiered lessons, students will get the work—work that is challenging but executable without frustration—just right daily. Students function differently. Some understand the lessons at a level above their skills; some may not understand at all and require tiered activities to complete the tasks.

Sample Tiered Assignments
- On different levels with adjusted challenges
- Focus on quality of work, not quantity
- Active learning for all students
- Engagement for all levels
- Aligned to objectives and goals
- Focused on the same skills

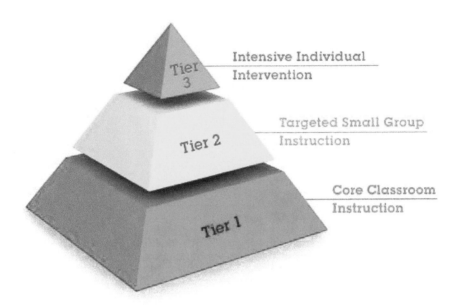

RTI (Response To Intervention)

3 Tiers of Support

(Tiered Instruction: Definition & Method, 2017)

Differentiation through Questioning

Brodsky (2020) stated that

> questioning has a rich and distinguished tradition in education. This disciplined practice of thoughtful questioning enables students to explore complex ideas. In the process, they uncover their implicit assumptions, expose deeply held beliefs, and recognize hidden contradictions. Rather than the teacher filling the mind of the student, both are responsible for moving the dialogue forward. (para. 3)

Look at the image below, and explain what you understand based on the picture.

Collier (2018) has argued that using effective questioning in the classroom brings many benefits as it:

- Encourages students to engage with their work and each other.
- Helps students to think out loud.
- Facilitates learning through active discussion.
- Empowers students to feel confident about their ideas.
- Improves speaking and listening skills.
- Builds critical thinking skills.
- Teaches respect for other people's opinions.
- Helps students to clarify their understanding.
- Motivates students and develops their interest in a topic.
- Allows teachers to check students' understanding.

The most famous questioning technique comes from Bloom's taxonomy:

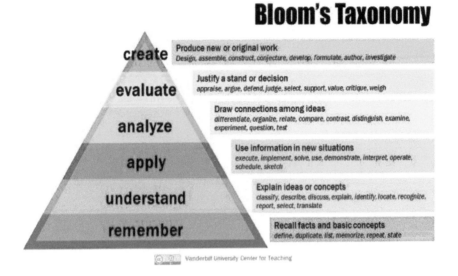

Bloom's Taxonomy

create — Produce new or original work
Design, assemble, construct, conjecture, develop, formulate, author, investigate

evaluate — Justify a stand or decision
appraise, argue, defend, judge, select, support, value, critique, weigh

analyze — Draw connections among ideas
differentiate, organize, relate, compare, contrast, distinguish, examine, experiment, question, test

apply — Use information in new situations
execute, implement, solve, use, demonstrate, interpret, operate, schedule, sketch

understand — Explain ideas or concepts
classify, describe, discuss, explain, identify, locate, recognize, report, select, translate

remember — Recall facts and basic concepts
define, duplicate, list, memorize, repeat, state

Vanderbilt University Center for Teaching

Armstrong (2010, p. 3) briefly explains the main categories of Taxonomy of educational goals as cited in the appendix of Taxonomy of Educational Objectives (Handbook One, pp. 201-207):

- **Knowledge** "involves the recall of specifics and universals, the recall of methods and processes, or the recall of a pattern, structure, or setting."
- **Comprehension** "refers to a type of understanding or apprehension such that the individual knows what is being communicated and can make use of the material or idea being communicated without necessarily relating it to other material or seeing its fullest implications."
- **Application** refers to the "use of abstractions in particular and concrete situations."
- **Analysis** represents the "breakdown of a communication into its constituent elements or parts such that the relative hierarchy of ideas is made clear, and the relations between ideas expressed are made explicit."

- **Synthesis** involves the "putting together of elements and parts to form a whole."
- **Evaluation** engenders "judgments about the value of material and methods for given purposes."
- (based on the work of Patricia Armstrong, former assistant director, Center for Teaching)

Differentiation through Metacognition

Drew (2020) has stated that "metacognition means thinking about thinking. John Flavell created the concept in the 1970s. It includes all the processes involved in regulating how we think" (p. 2). Drew provides examples including planning out one's work, tracking progress, and assessing one's knowledge.

Further, Short (2019) has explained, "metacognition, or thinking about how one thinks, is a useful skill for improving comprehension and learning" (p. 1) and "goes on to elaborate upon useful metacognition strategies for students" (p. 3):

- **Discussion**: Use notes and texts; explain the information to someone as if they have no prior knowledge of the topic.
- **Illustration**: Create pictures, mind maps, and diagrams of the information. Use color and creativity to spark creative ways to remember information.
- **Monologue**: Tell yourself the information in the mirror.
- **Songs**: Create a catchy tune to help remember important facts.
- **Write it out**: Rewrite all unknown information. Using various colors to organize ideas is helpful for some students.
- **Connections**: Write or draw connections between new information and facts/ideas that you understand. Make connections with your own life or current events.
- **Videos**: If there are relevant video clips about the topic, post them on Google Classroom for students to watch as part of their review process.

Drew (2020) has shared other strategies for metacognitive thinking. Metacognitive strategies are ones you can use to achieve your cognitive goals. These can include:

- **Self-questioning (internal talk)**: The ability to ask yourself questions when going through your work to ensure you are doing it to the best of your ability.
- **Meditation**: By pausing and clearing your mind, you can flush out all the extra chatter and focus well on the task.
- **Reflection**: As you work, reflect on what you are doing and think about ways to do it better. Schon called this "reflection-in-action."
- **Awareness of strengths and weaknesses**: Being aware of what tasks you are good at and what tasks you struggle with.
- **Awareness of learning styles**: Knowing which ways of learning best suit your skills. Learning styles are also known as "learning modalities" and include verbal, aural, kinesthetic, and tactile.
- **Use of mnemonic aids**: The ability to use rhymes, patterns, and associations to remember things. For example, when you meet someone new, you bank the knowledge in your mind by cognitively linking that person to another person with the same name.
- **Study skills**: Using study aids such as flash cards, spaced repetition, and other study strategies to remember.

Kiedaisch (2019) has stated that metacognition "involves five key thinking practices (para. 2)," or what the author used to describe to her students as "good habits of mind." They include:

1. Planning and goal-setting
2. Continual monitoring of progress
3. Identifying what you know
4. Identifying what you do not know
5. Adapting as necessary

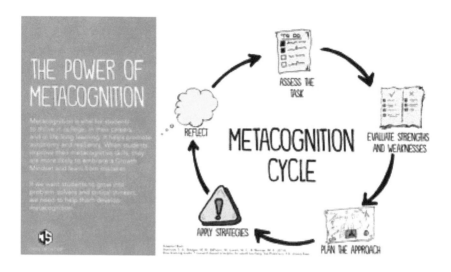

Differentiation through Grouping

A variety of groupings facilitate differentiation in a multilevel classroom (a combination of more than one grade level in a classroom), including *flexible and cooperative learning.*

Flexible Grouping

Cox (2020) has defined flexible grouping as "a range of grouping students together for delivering instruction. This can be as a whole class, a small group, or with a partner" (p. 1). Cox goes on to explain that "flexible grouping creates temporary groups that can last an hour, a week, or even a month. It is a temporary way for students to work together in a variety of ways and configurations depending upon activity and learning outcomes" (p. 1).

In order to successfully differentiate instruction through flexible grouping, teachers must consider student learning profiles. And in order to promote maximum learning, students need to move frequently among groups according to their specific needs. Wormeli (2020) has explained, "If it is time for some flexible grouping in our lessons, we can group according to many different factors and structures, including whole class or half class, teams, small groups, partners, triads, quads, one-on-one mentoring with an adult or peer, learning centers, online wiki groups, readiness, interest, and learner profile" (p. 1).

Brulles and Brown (2018) have articulated "five benefits of flexible grouping—*ongoing formative assessment, targeted instruction, focus on specific learning objectives, learner confidence, and differentiated curriculum and instruc*tion" (pp. 14–15).

The following are the details on the benefits of flexible grouping.

1. **Ongoing formative assessment**: Continual assessment is needed in a flexible grouping. Continual assessment relies on formal and informal assessment to structure and restructure flexible learning groups according to what the learners already know. When teachers use an ongoing assessment, they are constantly monitoring students' progress and identifying areas of intervention and support.

2. **Targeted instruction**: Assessment results provide teachers with data to analyze students' mastery and the needs of the lesson. When teachers can do flexible grouping for students based on assessments and data, they can purposely target instruction suited for the needs of each group of students.

3. **Focus on specific learning objectives**: Even though all the students in the class are learning the same topics in the class, the flexible group may have different objectives. The objectives created depend on the needs of each group.

4. **Learner confidence**: When students are grouped with similar peers, academic risk-taking significantly increases. The group becomes a safe place in which to provide instruction. Students will be more confident working on challenging but achievable learning goals. The assessment data collected helps the teachers in designing learning opportunities that build on students' readiness levels and interests.

5. **Differentiated curriculum and instruction**: When students are purposely grouped according to their interests and needs, teachers can efficiently structure their curriculum

and instruction to target students' needs within a group, class, or grade level.

Cooperative Learning

Zook (2018) has defined cooperative grouping as "the process of breaking a classroom of students into small groups so they can discover a new concept together and help each other," adding that "the core element of cooperative learning is to showcase the positive effects of interdependence while underlining the importance of personal responsibility" (p. 1).

Brame and Biel (2015) have further stated that cooperative learning is "characterized by positive interdependence, where students perceive that better performance by individuals produces better performance by the entire group. It can be formal or informal, but often involves specific teacher intervention to maximize student interaction and learning" (p. 1). The authors added that "it is infinitely adaptable, working in small and large classes and across disciplines, and can be one of the most effective teaching approaches available to college instructors" (p. 1).

Ways to Structure Cooperative Learning Grouping
Think-Pair-Share

The instructor asks a discussion question. Students are instructed to think or write about an answer to the question before turning to a peer to discuss their responses. Groups then share their responses with the class.

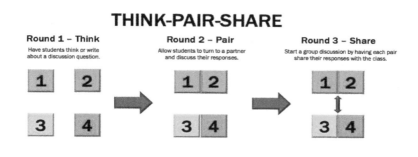

Jigsaw

In this approach, groups of students work in a team of four to become experts on one segment of new material, while other "expert teams" in the class work on other segments of new material. The class then rearranges itself, forming new groups that have one member from each expert team. The members of the new team then take turns teaching each other the material on which they are experts.

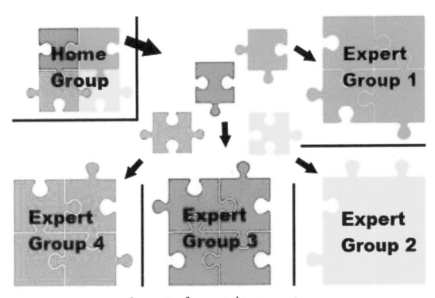

Strategies for special interventions

Peer Instruction

This modification of think-pair-share involves personal response devices (e.g., clickers). The question posted is typically a conceptual multiple-choice question. Students think about their answers and vote on a response before turning to a neighbor to discuss. Students can change their answers after discussion, and "sharing" is accomplished by the instructor revealing the graph of student response and using this as a stimulus for substantial class discussion. This approach is particularly well adapted for large classes.

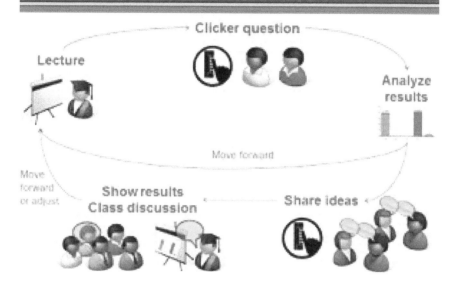

UNL Scientific Workshops

Differentiation through Materials and Resources

Multi-grade level classroom educators need to give emphasis on the different resources needed to support and maintain collaborative classroom which includes the use of authentic materials ant texts that improves inquiry and independent learning (Edu.gov, n.d.). Authentic materials students can use in the classroom such as pictures, songs, newspapers, movies, documentaries, advertisements, and pictures books.

- **Supplies for learning centers, workstations, and workshops**: Individual students may each have a clipboard or coil-bound notebook to use at learning centers and during workshops. Color-coded clipboards and folders are useful for managing cooperative learning groups. At many workstations, community supplies (e.g., pencils, pens, erasers, highlighters) are kept in tight containers.

- **Resources for mathematics and science investigations**: Collections of authentic materials (e.g., buttons, keys, bread-bag tags, seashells, beads, rocks, nests, grains, containers, small boxes) and artifacts play an important role in observing and communicating concepts. Combining authentic materials and commercial manipulatives (premade materials and can be purchased in stores) can enable a broad range of learners to work side by side to formulate a mathematical hypothesis or discover a scientific theory.
- **Art materials**: Readily available art materials are also necessary for a variety of learning styles, as well as supporting workshops for independent learners.
- **Text sets**: In the multilevel classroom, text sets are essential because they support a wide range of reading abilities and serve as instructional resources for reading, writing, and inquiry. Select a wide range of visual, print, and multimedia texts on a topic or theme from a content area that accommodates read-aloud, as well as shared, guided, and independent, reading. Text sets need to include developmentally and culturally appropriate expository and literary texts. (Building text sets based on content topics or genre studies may be a whole-school project over several years.)

  If students need support in reading a challenging text, they may join their cooperative group to listen while the "reader" reads the text aloud. For inquiry, students commonly choose challenging texts to read and view, and they often gain valuable information from these texts to share with the class or to answer their questions. Learning to read in the content areas is an essential reading skill; thus, text sets also need to include appropriate texts for strategic instruction in content reading. Resources and supplies need to be ready and accessible for several students who are engaged in a variety of learning tasks at one time.

Far and away, the best prize that life has to offer is the
chance to work hard at work worth doing.
—Theodore Roosevelt

Differentiation through Whole Group Instruction

Renaissance (2020) has stated that "whole-class instruction brings your classroom together as one large group. It is usually the time to introduce a new concept or encourage large-scale discussion" (p. 1). Furthermore, Meador (2019) has reported that "whole group instruction helps determine a baseline for learning and assessment. Teachers utilize the information gained from whole group instruction to plan for the future." The author goes on to state, "Teachers must conduct both informal and formal assessments as they move throughout a whole group lesson. Whole group instruction is most effective when it is immediately followed by small group instruction" (p. 2).

Teachers can differentiate whole group instruction by thinking of different ways to deliver the information. A one-size-fits-all curriculum does not meet all the needs of students (Davison, 2015). Using more than one method of instruction means students have more opportunities for learning. Alison (2018) has noted that whole group instruction "builds community, is more efficient than teaching the same skill over and over in small groups, and can be effective," adding that "questioning techniques need to be varied to meet the needs of the students, and the lesson objectives are geared toward the average students in the classroom" (p. 1).

The Thinker Builder (2017) suggested nine ways to differentiate whole group instruction:

1. Preteach to a small group
2. Arrange students' seating
3. Keep a visible record
4. Generate questions carefully
5. Be active during talks and turns
6. Provide more wait time

7. Utilize a student as an assistant
8. Vary an element
9. Allow a head start

Kelly (2018) has noted that whole group discussions or instructions "are an excellent instructional method when used in conjunction with other methods. Instruction should be varied from day to day to help reach the most students possible. Teachers will need to be good at managing and facilitating questions" (pp. 3–4). Furthermore, Adams and Pierce (2004) have stated that "flexible grouping arrangements such as pairs, triads, or quads, as well as whole-group and small-group instruction, create opportunities to meet individual needs" (p. 2).

Scaffold in Instruction

As a teacher, you do not wait for readiness to happen; you foster or "scaffold" it by deepening the child's powers at the stage where you find him or her now.—Jerome Bruner, *The Culture of Education*

One of the teaching strategies recommended for students is the use of scaffolding. It is important to use this strategy to help students learn the lesson in steps so that it is easily understood. Also, with the scaffold technique, the lesson is more geared toward being student-centered. Scaffolding is used as an instructional strategies as educators are asked to use 'scaffolding' teaching techniques to meet the state standards requirements so that learners can understand text complexity (Resilient Educator Editorial Team, 2020). Many of the students need scaffolding activities so that they can better grasp the concept or skill being taught. Teachers have to put in mind the relevance of the impact of scaffold activities when teaching students. The more the teacher scaffolds a lesson, the better is the success rate of the students' understanding of the lesson. Relatedly, Bennett (2019) has explained, "the origin of the word *scaffold* comes from Old French *eschace*, meaning 'a prop, support,' and instructional scaffolding may call to mind the kinds of wooden or steel supports one might see for workmen as they work around a building" (p. 2). If teachers do scaffold their lessons, students will learn better and gain confidence in learning. Scaffolding a lesson is necessary especially in a multi-grade level classroom with students having different learning styles and cognitive abilities.

> The IRIS Center (2005) has explained instructional scaffolding as a process through which a teacher adds support for students in order to enhance learning and aid in the mastery of tasks. The teacher does this by systematically building on students' experiences and knowledge as they are learning new skills. Just like the scaffold in the picture to the left, these supports are temporary and adjustable. As students master the assigned tasks, the supports are gradually removed. (p. 1)

Furthermore, Beth (2019) has stated that the aim of scaffolding is to ensure student's ability level is met by allowing them to individually grow in the process. Also, this allows for a logical patterns of progression and ensure support is in place until students display profieciently level. The goal is to ensure that students achieve the same learning skill but at a pace where lessons are scaffolded to understand the concept at a better condition. The Resilient Educator (2020) also noted that "scaffolding divides learning into steps, sometimes called 'chunks.' Students use the same texts but have tools to build on their knowledge throughout the learning process" (p. 1). The more teachers scaffold the lessons, the more students learn the concept and scaffolding may be decreased or can be fade away the moment the teachers notice students' academic progress and leans toward independence.

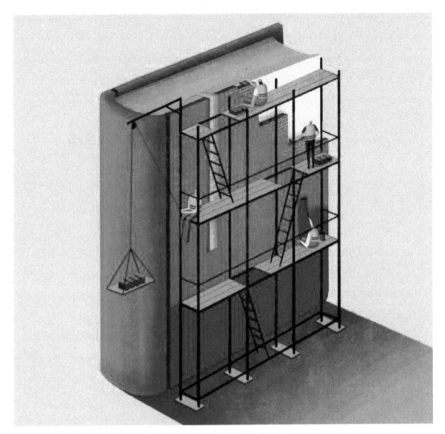

Ikon Images / Joseph Serra

Benefits of Scaffolding

Bennett (2019) has stated that instructional scaffolding provides improved opportunities for students to meet their learning goals and objectives. Instructional scaffolds can result in academic success, which increases motivation and engagement as scaffolding gives students practice on how to decrease complex processes into adaptable steps to be independent learners.

Batista et al. (2008) discuss various *benefits of scaffolding instructions*:
- Provides a welcoming and supportive learning environment
- Students feel free to ask questions and support one another through new learning
- The level of frustration is minimized for the learner

- Learners are engaged and motivated to learn
- The teacher who uses instructional scaffolding becomes more of a mentor and facilitator of knowledge, rather than the dominant expert of content.
- This teaching style allows the students to take a more active role in their learning.
- Scaffolding engages students in a meaningful and dynamic discussion.
- Students are challenged through deep learning and discovery.
- Scaffolding provides individualized instruction and, as a result, increases the likelihood that students will meet instructional objectives.
- Scaffolding programs can act as a possible early identifier of a student who is gifted and talented.
- There is greater assurance that the students will fully understand and acquire the desired skill, knowledge, or ability.
- Allows for a free-flowing lesson that is structured, focuses and where glitches have been minimized or eliminated before initiation
- Creates momentum within the classroom; students are on task, and less time is spent searching for information rather than learning and discovering.

Challenges in Scaffolding Instruction

Lipscomb et al. (n.d.) have discussed some challenges of scaffolding instruction:

- Very time-consuming
- Lack of sufficient personnel
- Potential for misjudging the zone of proximal development; success hinges on identifying the area that is just beyond but not too far beyond the students' abilities
- Inadequately modeling the desired behaviors, strategies, or activities because the teacher has not fully considered the individual student's needs, predilections, interests, and

abilities (such as not showing a student how to "double click" on an icon when using a computer)

- Full benefits are not seen unless the instructors are adequately trained
- Requires the teacher to give up control as fading occurs
- Lack of specific examples and tips in teacher's editions of textbooks

Examples of Instruction with and without Scaffolding Instruction

Example with scaffolding	Example without scaffolding
When I taught my daughter to ride her bike, I sat on the bike to demonstrate how to ride. I started her out with training wheels. Then I gradually raised the training wheels. Once she was ready to remove the training wheels, I steadied her with my hand and walked beside her, and only then did I let her take off on her own.	When I taught my daughter to ride her bike, I explained to her how to do it. Then I put her on the bike and gave her a shove.

(Adapted from audio by Robert Reid as cited in The IRIS Center)

Usually, teachers simply write or ask questions on the board, and students answer. Students with special needs sometimes just go through the motion of doing the task, but don't really grasp the reason of doing the assigned task. In this situation, it is important that teachers observe their students in order to see if the assigned tasks are understood or not. Scaffolding can be given to any subjects. Students can use this strategy with the guidance of the teachers in the classroom. Teachers can use observation, data, common sense, and teaching experience to enable better scaffolding techniques to students. Scaffolding instruction takes a lot of teacher modeling and guided practice. When students get stuck with a specific topic, it is essential to scaffold. According to the IRIS Center Covid-19 Resources (2021), there are different types of scaffolding. These are content scaffolding (lessons that are not so difficult or easy to do), task scaffolding (specifying tasks in steps and modeling), and material (use of written prompts or cues to help students do the tasks). Below is another example of how materials can be scaffolded to enable a student's clear understanding.

Example
(adapted from The IRIS Center Covid-19 Resources Vanderbilt University)

An example of material scaffolding is that, the teacher using the Capitalization, Overall Appearance, Punctuations, and Spelling (COPS) strategy, hangs a poster on the wall to display its steps. This poster serves as a guide for her students as they edit their papers. Once the students have shown mastery of using the strategy, the poster will be removed, but she will continue to prompt them to use the strategy throughout the year.

Forms of Scaffolding

Though scaffolding is primarily geared toward ELL (English Language Learners) students, it is also useful to all other students, with and without disabilities. Consistency is the key to utilizing the different forms of scaffolding instructions to assure the academic success of each student in the classroom. Huynh (2017) has stated that scaffolding supports students to enhance the skills that they can use and build upon in their future undertakings. Below is a graphic that describes different options for scaffolding instruction.

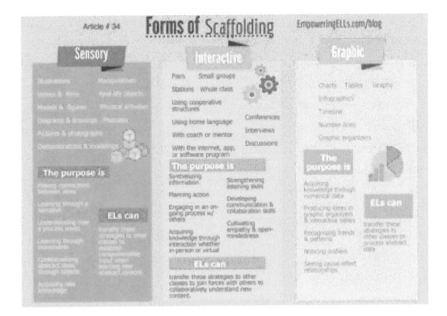

Prompts versus Scaffolds

Teachers use both prompts and scaffolds in teaching, yet there is a difference between them. Below is the graphic that shows the difference between the two.

Prompts vs. Scaffolds

A Prompt . . .	A Scaffold . . .
Leads students to notice what the teacher notices	Guides students to become aware of what there is to be noticed
Leads students to draw the same conclusions as the teacher from what they notice	Honors the conclusions students draw from what they notice
Does the thinking for the students	Allows students to do the thinking for themselves
Solves the problems for the students	Facilitates problem solving
Teaches the text	Teaches the thinking around the text

© Copyright 2012 by Dorothy Barnhouse and Vicki Vinton from What Readers Really Do (Portsmouth, NH: Heinemann)

Strategies for Scaffold Instruction

Sometimes students become discouraged and overwhelmed by lessons. But with proper guidance and instruction from the teacher, students can accomplish the learning goal. Mulvahill (2018) has stated that "scaffolding is a way to provide support for students by breaking learning down into manageable chunks as they progress toward stronger understanding and ultimately greater independence" (pp. 2–3). Below are Mulvahill's (2018) ten ways to scaffold learning for students:

1. Provide mini-lesson
2. Model or demonstrate
3. Describe concepts in various ways
4. Use visual aids
5. Give students think and talk time
6. Give students time to practice
7. Check for understanding during lessons
8. Activate prior knowledge
9. Front-load content-specific vocabulary concepts
10. Set them up for success

Three Approaches to Scaffolding Instruction

The IRIS Center (2005) has outlined three approaches for instructional scaffolding:

- **Content scaffolding**: This involves choosing content that is not hard or unfamiliar to keep the focus on the skill being taught. Instead, use familiar topics or engaging lessons, going from easy to more difficult.
- **Task scaffolding**: The teacher specifies the task or strategy to use and starts teaching through modeling of the lessons. In short, the teacher does a think-aloud and talks through each of the steps. Once the student understands the task, they can do it on their own while teachers observe their work, and as students cannot yet fully grasp the steps through the demonstrations, the teacher will continuously model while coaching students.

- **Material scaffolding:** This includes the use of written prompts or cues to assist students in performing specific tasks or strategies. Teachers may use cue sheets or guided examples as references to reduce frustration for students while performing a given task. Ideally the prompts and cues should be phased out over time as students master the steps of the task or strategy.

CHAPTER 5 DIVERSE AND INCLUSIVE CLASSROOM

Every student can learn, not on the same day, or in the same way.
—George Evans

Vanderbilt University

Cultural diversity and inclusion in the classroom have been increasing. Every year we see students of different background that we teach and interact with. The Drexel University School of Education (n.d.) has stated that as diversity and inclusion increases, it is significant to incorporate culturally responsive instruction to students. Diversity can include race, ethnicity, religions, socio-economic status, sexual orientation, gender identity, and language background. In order to deal with the rise of cultural diversity and inclusion, teachers have to be culturally responsible. Everyone must be able to deal with the diverse background in ways we feel we belong to each other. Teachers should teach lessons that incorporates diversity and inclusion. Lessons should also mirror of that with diverse background. Lessons can also be taken from a different source other than the usual texts the teachers use. The authors added that "diversity in and out of the classroom will continue to grow, so we must prepare students to adapt to an evolving world and embrace those different from themselves" (para. 2). Furthermore, Kampen (2019) has argued that "in an increasingly fragmented society, the ability to connect with peers, coworkers, and neighbors with diverse backgrounds and abilities is invaluable. Diversity improves critical-thinking skills, builds empathy, and encourages students to think differently" (p. 1). The more students are exposed to different texts in the classroom, the more students learn to understand the essence of the differences of the things that people see, read, use, and touch, and feel. Students deepen their understanding that there are many different people of different backgrounds out there other than their own. They will be able to discover the beauty of each other's differences.

The University of Delaware and American University (2020) define diversity and inclusion as follows:

1. Teaching to engage diversity, to include all learners, and to seek equity is essential for preparing civically engaged adults and for creating a campus and society that recognizes the contributions of all people.

2. Teaching for diversity refers to acknowledging a range of differences in the classroom. Teaching for inclusion signifies embracing difference.

3. Teaching for equity allows the differences to transform the way we think, teach, learn, and act such that all experiences and ways of being are handled with fairness and justice. 4. These ideas complement each other and enhance educational opportunities for all students when simultaneously engaged.

Diverse schools feature differences in ethnicity, socio-economic class, religion, reading level, athletic ability, background, gender, personality, and much more. An in-depth research review of dozens of other studies on diversity—conducted by The Century Foundation, a New York-based think tank—found that having different and divergent perspectives can create positive learning outcomes—it improves critical thinking skills, promotes creativity, and creates a culturally responsive community. (pp. 1–2)

What Does Instruction in an Inclusive Classroom Look Like?

As teachers, we strive to teach our students in ways we meet their individual needs regardless of their ability, background, skills, and status. Teachers also need to incorporate diverse lessons so that students understand different perspectives of the lesson being taught. "Inclusive teaching builds upon an instructor's basic instinct to ensure all voices are heard and that all students have a chance to participate fully in the learning process, by digging a little deeper into why participation imbalances exist" (Yale Poorvu Center for Teaching and Learning, 2020, p. 1). Furthermore, promoting cultural responsive education to teaching benefits all students. It supports students with different backgrounds and needs to become successful, encourages acceptance, and prepares students to survive in a diverse setting (Drexel University School of Education, n.d). There are many ways teachers can ensure that diverse and inclusive instruction is practiced in the classrooms. These approaches will help students strengthen their cultural responsiveness and fairness to others. Kampen (2019) has provided seven tips to encourage cultural diversity in classrooms:

1. **Examine your teaching materials**: Ensure that the instructional materials used for children are varied and address multicultural scenarios. Examine historical narratives and see what is missing. Survey your students on what kind of materials they like to have in the classroom. This

encourages critical thinking skills and creates an awareness among children of learning about other cultures.

2. **Get to know your students**: The students we have in our classroom are diverse, so as a teacher, use that reality to understand what they like. Use creative activities that utilize diversity in the school. Take your time to learn the diverse needs of your students. You can also ask the previous teachers of your students for background knowledge that might help you lead your classroom and better support the diverse needs of students.

3. **Be willing to address inequality**: Be proactive in addressing inequality in the classroom. Be fair in your treatment of your students. Effectively shut down any topics that risk causing a feeling of imbalance and encourage each student to include all of their peers in the classroom if you see division forming along, for example, racial or economic lines. The language used in the school should also promote equality to avoid gender bias or any form of discrimination against students' personal or socioeconomic status.

4. **Connect with parents and community**: Schools are part of the community, and parents are an integral part of schools. Celebrate diversity by inviting parents to attend school programs. Listen to parents' questions and concerns. Reach out to leaders in your community who can provide different perspectives. Also, encourage students to join community service learning projects in the school or their community so students see examples of diverse backgrounds. This inspires them as they look forward to their futures.

5. **Meet diverse learning needs**: Use different teaching approaches to address diverse learning needs. Use learning style surveys to differentiate lessons, do some project-based learning or even blended learning that encourages cooperation and participation among students in the classroom.

Ensure that there is active participation in classroom discussions and activities from all students at the school.

6. **Hire diversely**: Teachers work with people of different backgrounds, so you need to work on challenging your biases and assumptions about colleagues and students. Diversity of staff shows students various opportunities for learning as they are exposed to different learning styles and instruction.

7. **Support professional development opportunities**: Create professional development opportunities that encourage equality among members of the school community. Equip teachers with professional development that addresses challenges and removes biases and assumptions in themselves and their students.

What Are the Instructional Strategies of an Inclusive Classroom?

The Yale Poorvu Center for Teaching and Learning (2020) refers to inclusive teaching

> to pedagogy that strives to serve the needs of all students, regardless of background or identity, and support their engagement with subject material. Hearing diverse perspectives can enrich student learning by exposing everyone to stimulating discussion, expanding approaches to traditional and contemporary issues, and situating learning within students' contexts while exploring those contexts. (p. 1)

Furthermore, inclusive teaching strategies are intended to ensure "all students feel supported, learn freely, explore new ideas, freedom to express themselves, and are respected. Intentionally incorporating instructional strategies helps students view themselves as people who belong to the community of learners in a classroom and university" (University of Delaware, 2020, p. 2).

Parrish (2019) has suggested that using Universal Design for Learning (UDL) with all students can make classrooms more welcoming for students with special needs. Using UDL helps students to learn the content in many ways, provides different choices for learning, and provides accommodations for students with and without special needs.

Vogel (2016) has also supported the use of UDL, but she has added instructional strategies that make an inclusive classroom more engaging and teachers more knowledgeable about the students in the class.

1. **Identify your students' IEPs or 504 services**: Every teacher who serves students with special needs will receive a copy of their IEP, especially the accommodations, health plan, and behavior intervention plan. It is recommended that you read the IEP and other documents handed to you in their entirety. By doing so, you will be able to plan effective strategies to teach and provide support for this type of student in your classroom. The accommodations and the minutes to provide services are necessary for teachers to give the appropriate services in the classroom. Also, you are part of an IEP team meeting, so being knowledgeable about your students with special needs services helps you give the appropriate support. Place these IEP documents in a secure place. You can create a checklist of accommodations for the students you have in the classroom to ensure that you are providing the accommodations listed on the IEP.

2. **Support important life skills**: Most students with special needs lack the necessary basic skills in life. Which is to say, these kids struggle with honing their life skills. Skills such as telling time, writing a letter, opening a bottle, pouring water, writing their names, and even note-taking are harder to develop for these types of students. Teachers need to create an activity center in which these students can enhance their lacking skills. Teachers need to add life skills lessons to their daily schedule. Ensure that these skill activity enhancers are implemented with consistency so that the students develop their confidence and win over their weakness areas. To some, these life skills lessons are their future, so

do what you can to help the child achieve his or her full potential.

3. **Engagement in collaborative planning and teaching**: A teacher's classroom is open to all guests and visitors in the school. Opening up your room to different service providers, such as special education teachers, paraprofessionals, related service personnel, parents, and administrators, provides you with valuable opportunities for collaboration. Collaborative planning looks different at each school, but planning to meet with other professionals on the campus will help improve professional relationships and provide learning growth in other teaching strategies. Communication is vital to planning and teaching effectively. Ensure that the planning time set aside by the school is put toward progress and will produce explicit engagement.

4. **Development of a strong behavior management plan**: To ensure successful classroom instruction, it is essential to have a strong behavior management plan in place. Ensure that the classroom management expectations are accessible to all students. Classroom management rules should cater to the different needs of your students. One suggestion is to involve the students in creating their own classroom management rules to ensure that they are following the rules they made to the extent possible. Ensure that these classroom rules are visible for all students and guests when they are in your classroom. Some behavior management strategies that are effective in an inclusive classroom are classroom rules and expectations, daily classroom schedule, use of hand signals to inform students about noise, classroom work, and returning materials, behavior charts, rotation times, bathroom breaks, dismissal procedures, and recess time. These classroom management strategies need to be implemented with consistency to make an active classroom conducive to learning.

How Do Diverse Learners Come Together
in an Inclusive Environment?

McManis (2020) has encouraged the use of a variety of instructional formats:

> Start with whole-group instruction and transition to flexible groupings which could be small groups, stations/centers, and paired learning. About the whole group, using technology such as interactive whiteboards is related to high student engagement. Regarding flexible groupings: for younger students, these are often teacher-led, but for older students, they can be student-led with teacher monitoring. Peer-supported learning can be very effective and engaging and take the form of pair-work, cooperative grouping, peer tutoring, and student-led demonstrations. (p. 2)

CHAPTER 6: PARAPROFESSIONALS IN THE CLASSROOM: WHAT DO THEY DO AND WHO ARE THEY?

Para Professionals: an Important Part of the TEAM

Facilitated by Jen Farr, ONC BOCES

Paraprofessional: The heartfelt hero.
Using their talents to help students discover their own.
Dedicating their time and energy each day to the students in their care
and doing it all while meeting the individual needs of many.
—Theresa Kwant

Paraprofessionals are not certified teachers, but they play an essential role in the school's support staff. They are credentialed educators who work alongside and under the direction of a certified teacher or school professional. The Missouri Department of Elementary and Secondary Education has stated that "the term 'paraprofessional' is defined in the Every Student Succeeds Act (ESSA) and in the 2004 reauthorization of the Individuals with Disabilities Education Act (IDEA). ESSA says, The term "paraprofessionals," includes an instructional assistant in the classroom. IDEA allows "paraprofessionals who are appropriately trained and supervised, according to state and federal mandates, to assist in the provision of special education and related services. Each state is required to establish and maintain qualifications to ensure paraprofessionals' adequate training" (slide 6).

Furthermore, Patterson (2006) has written, "the No Child Left Behind (NCLB) Act (2001) requires that paraprofessionals work "under the direct supervision of a teacher" and "in close and frequent proximity to the teacher." The law also requires the supervising teacher to prepare lessons, plan instructional support services, and evaluate student achievement, tasks that very often are the responsibilities given to paraprofessionals in many schools today (Giangreco et al., 1997)" (p. 3).

Paraprofessionals often work one-on-one with those who receive special education and related services or those who have a 504 plan. Some paraprofessionals work with students in a special education classroom. Others work with students in a general education classroom or rotate to support all the classes in a specific grade level. Mauro (2020) has stated that "a paraprofessional also may be called a paraeducator, teaching assistant, instructional assistant, or aide. Informally, they may be referred to as a para pro or para," adding, paraprofessionals "must be good at working with kids, maintaining a positive and encouraging attitude, work closely with the teacher, able to work with parents, learn about the child's abilities and interests" (pp. 2-3). Often, "paraprofessionals learn these skills on the job as well as taking additional training throughout their careers" (pp. 2-3).

Relatedly, the United Federation of Teachers (2017) has reported:
> Paraprofessionals, including one-on-one paras, are entitled to a duty-free lunch period. A child's Individualized

Education Program can mandate paraprofessional coverage at lunch for that child, but the IEP cannot and does not specify a specific person to perform that role. If a para is asked to be with a child during the child's lunch, that para must still have a duty-free lunch period at some other point in the day. (If a para is unsure about the requirements on a child's IEP, he or she should ask to see the IEP. State law requires that paraprofessionals have access to the IEPs of students in their care.) (p. 2)

There are many definitions of "paraprofessional"; the graphic below describes what professionals do and how they support students with special education needs in the classroom.

Roles and Responsibilities of Paraprofessionals

Vierstra (2020) has noted four things a paraprofessional can provide in the classroom:

1. Instructional support
2. Language support
3. Behavioral support
4. Medical and physical support

Paraprofessionals can provide assistance in the classroom when it is deemed necessary. They are also called instructional assistants; however, the roles and responsibilities are the same. A paraprofessional can work one-on-one with a student, small group, or entire class. They can also provide extra support for the teacher during instruction. They can work collaboratively with the teacher in the classroom. They need to also know the content of the curriculum so they know how to support the students assigned to them.

According to Dr. Barry Ziff of the California State University Los Angeles Education Specialist Intern Program, instructional assistants can provide support in the following ways:

- Collaborative support during a lesson
- Small group instruction
- One-on-one assistance
- Prepare materials
- Grade student work
- Proximity support for appropriate discipline
- Sitting between two students to keep them focused
- Prepare bulletin boards
- Record grades
- Provide points, stickers, happy faces, etcetera
- Keep class supplies/materials organized
- Assist students with composition writing
- Correct homework, workbooks, etcetera
- Conduct daily classroom routines
- Restroom assistance
- Order supplies and materials

- Provide supervision during lunch, recess, breaks, etcetera
- Other duties as assigned by the teacher

In some circumstances, the paraprofessional is assigned to a specific child, but as long as the job description says "paraprofessional," the person is able to offer all kinds of instructional, language, behavior, medical, and physical support to the students they are serving.

How to Handle Conflicts between a Teacher and a Paraprofessional

Having an extra person in the classroom can be meaningful or challenging to special education or regular education teachers. While the extra support is much appreciated, it is inevitable that conflicts between two individuals arise. According to Edward and Taylor (2016), "a good working relationship between a teacher and a paraprofessional/educational assistant is essential to a supportive classroom that helps students learn both academically and behaviorally" (p. 1). No matter how proactive you are, issues may arise at certain points. Conflicts can be personal, professional, or simply involve a misunderstanding about who has responsibility for a certain student while paraprofessionals are in the classroom. They can also be about cultural differences, language barriers, time constraints, teaching styles, and expectations.

Like the regular or special education teacher who is bound to their duties, paraprofessionals also have certain duties and responsibilities. When conflicts arise, reporting the situation to the school administrator should be the last option. Basically, you want to stop the tension right there and then. Some would advise talking things out, setting expectations, being professional, and moving on, things that are easier said than done. But what do you do when this happens? Figure out if the paraprofessional has been given an orientation focused on dos and don'ts and expectations and lists of tasks. Remember this is a two-way approach and a win-lose situation.

The National Association of Special Education Teachers (NASET) (n.d., p. 5), has offered valuable knowledge and information about proper responses to a paraprofessional not performing well enough to meet the demands of the job:

- "Clarify job expectations for the paraprofessional. Review any written information (job description) that has been developed."
- "Document the paraprofessional's performance."
- "Develop a discrepancy analysis: How does the paraprofessional's performance differ from the established expectations? Do the expectations need to be clarified? Does the paraprofessional possess the knowledge/skills necessary to perform the task? Is additional training needed?"
- "Set clear expectations for improvement. Establish a timeline for evaluating results."
- "Document progress toward the goal." (p. 5)

Relatedly, Tapp (2017) has developed four tips for navigating working with paraprofessionals to avoid conflicts or issues in the classroom:

1. **Skip the snobbery**: Paraprofessionals are classified and trained individuals, and they deserve much respect. Avoid a feeling of competition as to who has more qualifications or seniority, and avoid making the other feel inferior. This is not just unhealthy but also affects the students' learning. The key is to work as a team.

2. **Communicate effectively**: Teachers need to communicate to their support person in the classroom what they want and how the classroom should be managed. It is ideal to set expectations for both at the beginning of the school year and revisit these expectations when needed. Be clear about who does the instruction, who brings the kids to the restroom, recess, cafeteria, or if in case a school activities. Also, inform your aides what will be expected of them if there is an IEP meeting scheduled. Being clear about expectations helps both individuals better understand each other's roles and responsibilities.

3. **Plan with your paraprofessional**: Always include the paraprofessional in your plans. Ignoring this task not only causes trouble but also makes your aides feel inferior and alone. Paraprofessionals have skills and talents they can share with you. Letting them share their expertise makes your life easier.

4. **Share resources and results**: It is important for your paraprofessional attends the confidentiality training provided at your school as well. This is because there is information that can only be shared with certain individuals. Other information, such as grades, test results, and lesson plans, is OK to share generally. You want your aide will know how to support the students assigned to them. The more you share resources and results with your aides, the less chaos there will be. This is a win-win situation.

Additionally, Fitzell (2021) has shared some important ways to avoid conflicts with your paraprofessional in the classroom: "provide the paraprofessional with lesson plans, activities, or 'to-do' items as soon as possible; avoid interruption when the paraeducator is working with a student or several students; interruption undermines the paraprofessional's authority which causes distress and possible conflict" (p. 2). Fitzell (2021) added to provide paraprofessional "with a binder that contains class rules, expectations, a syllabus, class schedule, breaks, and other important information; and model/teach how to respond to specific behavior" (p. 2). Doing this can help both the teacher and the paraprofessional work seamlessly.

The key here is to make sure both adults in the classroom understand their roles and responsibilities—and understand that their students are the true winners if both share responsibility equally as a team!

FREQUENTLY ASKED QUESTIONS

Never doubt that a small group of committed people can
change the world: indeed it is the only thing that ever has.
—Margaret Mead

Though every state handles IEP meetings and implementing special education services slightly differently, the following questions broadly apply.

- **What information should be used for an IEP?** Student profile, parent/guardian information, prereferral, current evaluation data entered in the web database by a designated web-based data person before an IEP meeting, other district-based curriculum data, grades, state test results, and additional information from related service personnel

- **When can the IEP be called official?** An IEP is not official until an IEP team meeting is conducted. Any IEPs that have not been held yet are in draft mode. After the parent signs the form and all information and changes are entered into the computer, the IEP can be made official by an ODR. An amendment to the IEP can be completed for any changes.

- **What is the difference between an amendment and a new IEP?** If there are any changes made to the officially signed IEP, all procedural safeguards must be followed. A new review IEP is completed on an annual basis, and an IEP can be amended as many times as needed afterward.

- **Will the web-based system "auto-check" the general student information after I add a new educational need area?** No. It will show up when you click "validation" on the IEP.

- **Will adding a new state testing accommodation before the accommodations automatically update the accommodations?** No. You need to go back to the accommodations page to ensure that the appropriate statewide testing accommodations are rechecked. Some states might not have distinct lists of accommodations.

- **What justifications are needed for LRE?** Justification is required if the placement is 80 percent or above in the special education setting.

- **Can you use the second time frame for a child moving from the three-to-five to the six-through-twenty-one settings?** Yes, you can add a second time frame depending on the need for the time frame.

- **When is the site determination page completed for an IEP?** The site determination should be completed within ten days. It can also be done during an IEP team meeting.

- **Is spell check run on the entire document?** Spell check is completed page by page; however, make sure to check IEPs for grammatical errors and any missing information before printing. It is advisable that you ask your instructional specialist to double-check your IEP at least two weeks before the IEP meeting.

- **What keeps a teacher from amending an IEP when it is in review and changing everything?** You need to keep the original date of the IEP, the ODR signature date, parent signature date, and other IEP participants' dates. A teacher may amend an IEP until the anniversary date or develop a new IEP at any time. Follow the process of amending the IEP. The ODR must make the IEP official.

- **Is the amendment history saved on the computer?** Yes. An amendment history is automatically saved on the computer. You can place this form in the student's IEP folder as well.

- **How are the short-term objectives identified for the extended school year program?** There is a box or space on the IEP where you type the short-term goals. Short-term goals are still SMART goals.
- **Must an ODR be identified in the IEP participants?** Yes. It is essential to identify the ODR for an IEP. A certain member of the personnel from the special education department is assigned as an ODR; however, in their absence, the school must assign an ODR to sign. An ODR must be present in the IEP meeting to sign and make the document official.
- **Can the review IEP be made official if the parent does not attend the IEP meeting?** Yes. The parent signature line indicates that the parent did not participate in the conference. You can submit the IEP as official. Sometimes, parents are working or caught up with other pressing priorities, and they cannot attend the meeting in person; an alternative is to conduct an IEP via phone conference. Just state under the parent section that the meeting has been held via phone conference or via an online platform. However, a parent must attend if the IEP is initial or interim.
- **Can the review IEP be made official if the parent refuses to sign the IEP?** Yes. In the parent section, indicate the parent declined to sign the IEP and submit it to make the IEP official.
- **Can the review IEP be made official if the parent is taking the district to due process?** The due process IEPs are the review IEPs. These IEPs must be processed as approved IEPs. In the parent signature field, enter notes indicating the due process and other pertinent information and dates.
- **Does the alternate assessment require objectives?** Yes, IDEA requires short-term objectives for students

participating in the alternative assessment with alternative academic levels.

- **Do you need to list strengths and weaknesses on the GSI page?** Yes, you are required to list both strengths and weaknesses. Then, that information will be repeated when you are writing the present level of performance under the instructional page of the IEP for each core subject area entered.

- **If the boxes under the educational needs are checked more than once, should a goal be made for each one?** Yes, it is required that the number of boxes checked under the educational need area also be the number of goals written for the student.

- **If an eighth-grader takes the statewide assessment and does not pass, can the child's IEP be changed to alternative testing, and can the student be promoted to the next grade level?** No. The student must follow the promotion criteria for the assessment taken in the spring. A student must meet alternative assessment participation criteria to be eligible to take the test.

- **How many exit documents need to be checked for high school students?** A student need pursue only one exit document.

- **Are the itinerant vision and itinerant hearing considered to be IEP participants?** Yes, but they are considered special education teachers. They can put their title on the original IEP if they participate.

- **Is it necessary to amend an IEP when a student turns six during the school year?** No. For child count purposes, the students are reported in the appropriate LRE setting.

- **How do I address IEP goals?** Use state-aligned standards and goals that are SMART-specific, measurable, attainable, results-oriented, and time-bound. Also, look at the specific learning needs of your students with disabilities who are struggling so you can tie both the skills and the standards together to write a SMART goals IEP.

- **Who facilitates an IEP meeting?** This varies from district to district and school to school, but usually the student's IEP teacher conducts an IEP meeting.
- **Can parents request an IEP meeting?** Yes, parents have the right to request an IEP at any time it is needed.
- **Can an IEP meeting be rescheduled?** Yes, as long as the meeting date is within the timeline to avoid being out of compliance.
- **Who makes the IEP official?** Only the official designated representative is allowed to make the IEP official. A special education teacher or any other IEP participant cannot make it official unless you are assigned as an ODR.
- **Can IEP information be erased using a correction fluid?** No. It is prohibited to use correction fluid on an IEP document. When correcting a piece of information in an IEP, you can strike through a line, but never use correction fluid.

A Final Word: Tips to Enjoy the Journey

Wow! There is so much information in this book. I hope that you were able to learn and gain insights into special education—what it is, the laws, differentiation, inclusion and diversity, roles and responsibilities of your paraprofessional in the classroom, and most important of all, how to conduct an IEP meeting. My advice is to take things one step at a time. Being a new special education teacher, paraprofessional, or other special education professional can be daunting and overwhelming. But know that there is hope. Seek help from other professionals who may have knowledge of what you are yearning to learn. It is OK to ask for support. If you want to learn, be coachable. Read about and research what you want to learn. Do not be afraid to learn. It always starts with little things, and before you know it, you are an expert in the things that you believed you did not know at first. Take small steps, be humble, and keep on learning.

Like I mentioned at the beginning of this book, this text is meant to serve as a resource. You can combine the information gained from this book with your stock knowledge. May this help answer some of your questions and provide you with some wisdom. Thank you for your support, and happy reading!

REFERENCES

1+1+1=1. (n.d.). *Differentiated instruction image.* https://1plus1plus1equals1.net/wp-content/uploads/2018/11/Differentiated-Instruction-Resources.png.

Adams, C., & Pierce, R. (2004). Tiered lessons: One way to differentiate mathematics instruction. *Gifted Child Today, 27*(2), 50–65. https://www.davidsongifted.org/search-database/entry/a10513.

Ambrose, S. A., Bridges, M. W., Di Pietro, M., Lovett, M. C., & Norman, M. K. (2010). *How learning works: 7 research-based principles for smart teaching.* Jossey-Bass.

Alison. (2018, November 3). *How to differentiate your kindergarten reading instruction when your students have a big range of abilities.* Learning at the Primary Pond. https://learningattheprimarypond.com/blog/how-to-differentiate-in-kindergarten/.

Arkansas State University (2016). *What is the teacher's role in IEPs?* https://degree.astate.edu/articles/k-12-education/what-is-the-teachers-role-in-ieps.aspx.

Arkansas State University (2019, June 3). *What is the range of special education students' disabilities?* https://degree.astate.edu/articles/k-12-education/what-is-the-range-of-special-education-students-disabilities.aspx.

Armstrong, P. (2010). *Bloom's Taxonomy.* Vanderbilt University Center for Teaching. Retrieved [March 7, 2022] from https://cft.vanderbilt.edu/guides-sub-pages/blooms-taxonomy/.

Autism Speaks. (n.d.). *What is autism?* https://www.autismspeaks.org/what-autism.

Bajrami, I. (2013). The importance of differentiation in supporting diverse learners. *Journal of Education and Practice, 4*(22), 149–154. https://www.iiste.org/Journals/index.php/JEP/article/viewFile/8339/8675.

Barnhouse, D., & Vinton, V. (2012). *Prompts vs. scaffold image.* https://tomakeaprairie.files.wordpress.com/2012/06/prompt-vs-scaffold-2.png?w=584.

Batista, R., Bonner, C., & Halls, C. (2008). *Benefits and challenges of scaffolding.* Scaffolding Literacy. https://scaffoldingliteracy.weebly.com/benefits-and-challenges-of-scaffolding.html.

Baumel, J. (2014). *What is an IEP?* GreatSchools. https://www.greatschools.org/gk/articles/what-is-an-iep/.

Bennett, C. (2020, February 11). *How scaffolding instruction can improve comprehension.* ThoughtCo. https://www.thoughtco.com/ways-to-scaffold-instruction-in-grades-7-12-4147435.

Best, J. (2020, June 23). *A teacher's guide to differentiation.* 3P Learning. https://www.3plearning.com/blog/differentiated-instruction/.

Biel, R., & Brame, C. J. (2015). *Setting up and facilitating group work: Using cooperative learning groups effectively.* Vanderbilt University Center for Teaching. https://cft.vanderbilt.edu/guides-sub-pages/setting-up-and-facilitating-group-work-using-cooperative-learning-groups-effectively/.

B. I. G. Solutions. (2017). *13 Categories of disability under IDEA law.* https://behavioralinspiredgrowth.com/special-ed-resources/categories-disability-idea-law/.

Bloom, B.S. et al. (2014). *Taxonomy of education objectives: the classification of educational goals.* New York. Longman, c1984.

Bloom's Taxonomy. (n.d.). *What is Bloom's Taxonomy?* https://www.bloomstaxonomy.net/.

Blue Mango. (2017). *3 tiers of support image.* http://www.bluemangollc.com/wp-content/uploads/2015/05/RTI_3_tiers.jpg

BrainyQuote. (n.d.). *Margaret Mead quote.* https://www.brainyquote.com/quotes/margaret_mead_100502.

Bright Hub Education. (2009, May 26). *Age eligibility and student coverage under IDEA.* https://www.brighthubeducation.com/special-ed-law/36708-age-eligibility-for-student-coverage-under-idea/.

Bright Hub Education. (2020, February 15). *Different learning styles in the classroom.* https://www.brighthubeducation.com/teaching-methods-tips/64037-learning-styles-in-the-classroom/.

Brodksy, J. (2020). *Why questioning is the ultimate skill.* https://www.forbes.com/sites/juliabrodsky/2021/12/29/why-questioning-is-the-ultimate-learning-skill/?sh=38115136399f

Brown, K., & Brulles, D. (2018). *A Teacher's guide to flexible grouping and collaborative learning.* Free Spirit Publishing. https://www.freespirit.com/files/original/Flexible-Grouping-Collaborative-Learning-preview-1.pdf.

Camp Verde Schools. (2014). *Learning knows no bounds image.* http://campverdeschools.org/wp-content/uploads/2014/05/kids-special-education.gif.

Causton, J. (2014). *A new paraprofessional job description: How to really support a child graphic.* https://i.pinimg.com/564x/e0/07/9d/e0079de254853d1934dbf8bb48b365d9.jpg.

Central Dauphin School District. (n.d.). *Special education image.* https://www. cdschools.org/cms/lib04/PA09000075/Centricity/Domain/24/Special%20 Ed.PNG.

Chick, N. (2010). *Learning styles.* Vanderbilt University Center for Teaching. https://cft.vanderbilt.edu/guides-sub-pages/learning-styles-preferences/.

Chris, D. (2021, November 13). *Metacognitive theory definition pros and cons.* Helpful Professor. https://helpfulprofessor.com/metacognitive-theory/.

Collier, E. (2020, December 31). *What is effective questioning & why should I use it in my classroom?* High Speed Training. https://www.highspeedtraining. co.uk/hub/what-is-effective-questioning/.

Columbia University Office of Work/Life. (n.d.). *Early intervention & special education.* Columbia University. https://worklife.columbia.edu/content/ early-intervention-special-education.

Cook, L. (2004, April 24). *Co-teaching: Principles, practices, and pragmatics.* New Mexico Public Education Department Quarterly Special Education Meeting. https://files.eric.ed.gov/fulltext/ED486454.pdf.

Cox, J. (2014, September 9). *Flexible grouping as a differentiated strategy.* TeachHUB. http://www.teachhub.com/ flexible-grouping-differentiated-instruction-strategy.

Curry School of Education and Human Development. (2017, August 10). *Faculty conversation: Carol Tomlinson on differentiation.* University of Virginia. https://curry.virginia.edu/news/ faculty-conversation-carol-tomlinson-differentiation.

Dalien, S. (n.d.). *Self-contained classroom defined.* Special Ed Resource. https:// specialedresource.com/resource-center/self-contained-classroom-defined.

Davison, S. (2015). *Differentiate your direct instruction: Make content accessible to all students.* Teaching Channel. https://learn.teachingchannel.com/ blog/2015/05/14/differentiate-your-direct-instruction/#:~:text=You%20can%20 differentiate%20your%20whole%20group%20instruction%20by,will%20 have%20more%20than%20one%20opportunity%20to%20understand.

Edward, M., & Taylor, J. (2016). *5 ways to improve relationships with educational assistants & paraprofessionals.* Crisis Prevention Institute. https://www. crisisprevention.com/Blog/working-relationships.

EL Education. (n.d.). *Helping all learners: Tiering.* https://eleducation.org/resources/ helping-all-learners-tiering.

Farr, J. (n.d.). *Paraprofessionals: An important part of the team image.* https://i.pinimg. com/originals/09/0d/e9/090de919f5ca8ab5d94cc9d6d33514d2.jpg.

Grand Canyon University. (2020, May 28). *How to recognize and support learning styles in the classroom.* https:// www.gcu.edu/blog/teaching-school-administration/ how-recognize-and-support-learning-styles-classroom.

Griend, M. V. (2019, August 12). *Conducting case conferences.* South Bend Community School Corporation. http://www.sped.sbcsc.k12.in.us/ppm/conductingieps.html.

Huebner, T. A. (2010). *What research says about differentiated learning.* ASCD. http://www.ascd.org/publications/educational-leadership/feb10/vol67/num05/Differentiated-Learning.aspx.

Huynh, T. (2017, April 14). *Three types of scaffolding: There's a scaffold for that.* TanKHuyhn. https://www.empoweringells.com/scaffolding-instruction/.

Iowa IDEA Information. (2021). *Interim IEPs.* Types of IEPs (iowaideainformation.org)

IRIS Center. (2005). *Providing instructional supports: Facilitating mastery of new skills.* Vanderbilt University. https://iris.peabody.vanderbilt.edu/module/sca/.

IRIS Center Covid-19 Resources. (2021). *How do I scaffold instruction?* Vanderbilt University. IRIS | Page 2: How Do I Scaffold Instruction? (vanderbilt.edu)

IRIS Center Covid-19 Resources. (2021). *Material scaffolding.* Vanderbilt University. https://iris.peabody.vanderbilt.edu/module/sca/cresource/q2/p05/#content

Kampen, M. (2019, April 17). *7 ways to support diversity in the classroom.* Prodigy. https://www.prodigygame.com/blog/diversity-in-the-classroom/.iowa

Kansas University Department of Special Education. (n.d.). *Instructional accommodations.* Kansas University. http://www.specialconnections.ku.edu/~kucrl/cgibin/drupal/?q=instruction/instructional_accommodations.

Kiedaisch, J. (2018, June 11). *What is metacognition? A guide for educators.* We Are Teachers. https://www.weareteachers.com/what-is-metacognition/.

Kelly, M. (2018, March 1). *Whole group discussions pros and cons.* ThoughtCo. https://www.thoughtco.com/whole-group-discussion-pros-and-cons-8036.

Lam, K. (2017, October 9). *How to engage the 7 types of learners in your classroom.* Literacy Planet. https://www.literacyplanet.com/au/news/engage-7-types-learners-classroom/.

Lewis, B. (2020, February 11). *Scaffolding instruction strategies.* ThoughtCo. https://www.thoughtco.com/scaffolding-instruction-strategies-2081682.

Lightner, L. (2020, March 7). *40 IEP goals for reading. Comprehension strategies. Evaluations.* A Day In Our Shoes. 40 IEP Goals for Reading | Comprehension | Strategies | Evaluations | A Day in our Shoes

Linde, S. *Tiered instruction: definition & method.* (2017, April 27). https://study.com/academy/lesson/tiered-instruction-definition-method.html.

Lipscomb, L., Swanson, J., & West, A. (n.d.). *Scaffolding.* Granite State College. https://granite.pressbooks.pub/teachingdiverselearners/chapter/scaffolding-2/.

Loving2Learn. (n.d.). *Learning styles image.* Retrieved June 24, 2020, from http://tofigamammadova.weebly.com/uploads/1/6/9/6/16961478/735522976.png?824.

Lucas, A., & Walsh, S. (n.d.). *Procedural safeguards: Family rights, confidentiality, and dispute resolution.* Early Childhood Technical Assistance Center. https://ectacenter.org/topics/procsafe/procsafe.asp.

Malvik, C. (2020). *4 types of learning styles: How to accommodate a diverse group of students.* Rasmussen University. https://www.rasmussen.edu/degrees/education/blog/types-of-learning-styles/.

Mauro, T. (2020, May 4). *Understanding the paraprofessional's role in the classroom.* Verywell Family. https://www.verywellfamily.com/what-is-a-paraprofessional-3106873.

McManis, L. D. (n.d.). *Inclusive education: What it means, proven strategies, and a case study.* Resilient Educator. https://resilienteducator.com/classroom-resources/inclusive-education/.

Meador, D. (2019, June 23). *Exploring the value of the whole group differentiation in the classroom.* ThoughtCo. https://www.thoughtco.com/exploring-the-value-of-whole-group-instruction-3194549.

Missouri Department of Elementary and Secondary Education. (n.d.). *Paraprofessional roles & responsibilities Power Point Presentation.* [PowerPoint Slides]. Paraprofessional Roles & Responsibilities Power Point Presentation | Missouri Department of Elementary and Secondary Education (mo.gov)

Morin, A. (n.d.). *Early intervention.* What Is Early Intervention? | Understood - For learning and thinking differences

Mulvahill, E. (2018, August 31). *10 ways to scaffold learning.* We Are Teachers. https://www.weareteachers.com/ways-to-scaffold-learning/.

National Association of Special Education Teachers. (2012). *Working with paraprofessionals in your school: Solving performance and interpersonal problems.* https://writesolutions.org/wp-content/uploads/2012/11/Solving_Performance_and_Interpersonal_Problems1.pdf.

Nieves, K. (2020, April 16). *8 tips for conducting virtual IEP meetings.* George Lucas Educational Foundation. https://www.edutopia.org/article/8-tips-conducting-virtual-iep-meetings.

PACER National Parent Center on Transition and Employment. (2019). *The Individuals with Disabilities Act (IDEA) and secondary transition.* PACER. https://www.pacer.org/transition/learning-center/laws/idea.asp.

Pangatungan, M. (2018). *The impact of read-aloud accommodations of fourth- and fifth-grade elementary students with and without learning impairment: A descriptive case study.* [Doctoral dissertation, Concordia University]. https://commons.cu-portland.edu/edudissertations/163.

Patterson, K. B. (2006). Roles and responsibilities of paraprofessionals: In their own words. *TEACHING Exceptional Children Plus, 2*(5), article 1. Roles and Responsibilities of Paraprofessionals: In Their Own Words (ed.gov)

Parrish, N. (2019, May 15). *Ensuring that instruction is for inclusive and diverse learners*. George Lucas Educational Foundation. https://www.edutopia. org/article/ensuring-instruction-inclusive-diverse-learners.

Partners Resource Network. (n.d.). *Annual IEP review meeting*. https://prntexas.org/ annual-iep-review-meeting/.

Personalized Learning for All. (2016). *All children can learn image*. http://personalizedlearningforall.com/wp-content/ uploads/2016/07/1405530391.png.

Preceden. (n.d.). *History of special education*. Retrieved [March 8, 2022] from file:/// home/chronos/u-5b5a3fbd63d308 67ff50af057977b19787c07204/ MyFiles/Downloads/history_of_special_education.pdf

Province of Manitoba Education. (n.d.). *Differentiation in the multilevel classroom*. https://www.edu.gov.mb.ca/k12/docs/support/multilevel/chap4.pdf.

Renaissance. (n.d.). *Whole-class instruction*. https://www.renaissance.com/edwords/ whole-class-instruction/.

Resilient Educator Editorial Team. (n.d.). *Three scaffolding techniques to enhance common core standards learning*. Resilient Educator. https:// resilienteducator.com/classroom-resources/three-scaffolding-techniques-to-enhance-common-core-standards-learning/.

Resnick, B. (2009). *Understanding the IEP process: A six-step guide*. Rush Neurobehavioral Center. http://rnbc.org/2009/10/ understanding-the-iep-process-a-six-step-guide/.

Robb, L. (n.d.). *What is differentiated instruction?* Scholastic Teacher Resources. https://www.scholastic.com/teachers/articles/teaching-content/ what-differentiated-instruction/.

Rogers, A. (2017, April 24). *How to differentiate in math*. Sciencing. https:// sciencing.com/methods-of-teaching-mathematics-in-primary-school-12745838.html.

Rosen, P. (n.d.). *Special education: Federal law vs. state law*. Understood. https://www.understood.org/en/school-learning/your-childs-rights/ basics-about-childs-rights/special-education-federal-law-vs-state-law.

School of Education at American University. (2019, July 24). *The benefits of inclusion and diversity in the classroom*. American University. https://soeonline.american.edu/blog/ benefits-of-inclusion-and-diversity-in-the-classroom.

Schwartz, S. (2018, December 5). *What does it take to make co-teaching work?* EducationWeek. https://www.edweek.org/ew/articles/2018/12/05/what-it-takes-to-make-co-teaching-work.html.

Short, K. (2019, July 17). *Study strategies beyond memorization*. George Lucas Educational Foundation. https://www.edutopia.org/article/ study-strategies-beyond-memorization.

Smith, D. (2018, June 25). *Advantages & disadvantages of different learning styles.* Classroom. https://classroom.synonym.com/advantages-disadvantages-different-learning-styles-2873.html.

Special Education Degrees. (n.d.). *What are inclusive special education programs?* https://www.special-education-degree.net/what-are-inclusive-special-education-programs/.

Special Education Guide. (n.d.). *Disability profiles.* https://www.specialeducationguide.com/disability-profiles/.

Special Education Guide. (n.d.). *The IEP process explained.* https://www.specialeducationguide.com/pre-k-12/individualized-education-programs-iep/the-iep-process-explained/.

SpecialEdNews. (n.d.). *Least restrictive environment.* http://www.specialednews.com/special-education-dictionary/lre---least-restrictive-environment.htm.

Spencer, L. (2018). *The power of metacognition image.* https://www.spencerauthor.com/wp-content/uploads/2018/08/metacognition-benefits.png.

Strategies for Special Interventions. (n.d.). *Jigsaw instruction strategy image.* http://strategiesforspecialinterventions.weebly.com/uploads/3/8/7/5/38759681/_8034395.jpg?457.

Tapp, F. (2017, July 6). *A teacher's guide to working with paraprofessionals.* We Are Teachers. https://www.weareteachers.com/working-with-paraprofessionals/.

Teach.com. (2020, August). *Learning styles all students are created equally and (differently).* https://teach.com/what/teachers-know/learning-styles/.

The Thinker Builder. (2017). *9 ways to differentiate your whole group instruction.* https://www.thethinkerbuilder.com/2017/01/9-ways-to-differentiate-your-whole.html.

Timetoast. (n.d.). *History of SPED timeline.* https://www.timetoast.com/timelines/history-of-sped-timeline.

Tomlinson, C. A., & Strickland, C. A. (2005). *Differentiation in practice: A resource guide for differentiating curriculum, grades 9–12.* ASCD.

Torrey, R. (n.d.). *Why image.* https://i.pinimg.com/originals/3f/5d/58/3f5d58630effcb26fb77818e8dc9d450.jpg.

UnderstandingSpecialEducation.com (n.d.). *Understanding the 13 categories of special education.* https://www.understandingspecialeducation.com/13-categories-of-special-education.html.

Understood Team. (n.d.). *The IEP meeting: An overview.* Understood. https://www.understood.org/en/school-learning/special-services/ieps/the-iep-meeting-an-overview.

University of Delaware Center for Teaching & Assessment of Learning. (n.d.). *Diversity and inclusive teaching.* University of Delaware. https://ctal.udel.edu/resources-2/inclusive-teaching/.

US Department of Education. (2015). *Every Student Succeeds Act*. https://www.ed.gov/essa?src=rn.

US Department of Education. (2021). *Family Education Rights and Privacy Acts (FERPA)*. https://www2.ed.gov/policy/gen/guid/fpco/ferpa/index.html.

US Department of Education (2017, May 2). *Special education*. https://sites.ed.gov/idea/regs/b/a/300.39.

United Federation of Teachers. (2017, December 6). *Paraprofessional's responsibilities*. https://www.uft.org/news/you-should-know/know-your-rights/paraprofessionals-responsibilities-0.

UNL Scientific Teaching Workshops. (n.d.). *Peer instruction image*. https://sites.google.com/site/unlscientificteachingworkshops/_/rsrc/1468886507620/scientific-teaching/peer-instruction/PI.png?height=292&width=400.

Vanderbilt University Center for Teaching (n.d.). *Bloom's Taxonomy image*. https://cft.vanderbilt.edu/wp-content/uploads/sites/59/Bloomtaxonomy-e1445435495371.jpg.

Vanderbilt University (2017). *Diversity and inclusion image*. https://news.vanderbilt.edu/2017/01/20/series-of-training-around-issues-of-diversity-and-inclusion-offered-to-vanderbilt-community/diversity-and-inclusion-graphic/

Vanderbilt University Center for Teaching. (n.d.). *Think-pair-share image*.https://live.staticflickr.com/7846/40507414413_e1c930d544_b.jpg.

Vierstra, G. (n.d.). *Paraprofessionals: What you need to know*. Understood. https://www.understood.org/en/school-learning/for-educators/learning-and-thinking-differences-basics/paraprofessionals-what-you-need-to-know.

Virginia Department of Education. (2019). *Standards-based IEP Sample measurable goals math K–12 2016 standards of learning*. http://www.doe.virginia.gov/special_ed/iep_instruct_svcs/stds-based_iep/sample-goals-math.pdf.

Vogel, K. (2016, January 4). *5 effective strategies for an inclusive classroom*. KQED. https://www.kqed.org/education/75955/5-effective-strategies-for-the-inclusive-classroom.

Watson, S. (2019, March 24). *How to write IEP goals: Writing SMART goals*. ThoughtCo. https://www.thoughtco.com/how-to-write-iep-goals-3110987.

Watson, S. (2019, November 18). *Introduction to special education resource rooms*. ThoughtCo. https://www.thoughtco.com/special-education-resource-room-3110962.

Webster, J. (2019, July 3). *Self-contained classrooms: Self-contained classrooms supporting students with significant disabilities*. ThoughtCo. https://www.thoughtco.com/self-contained-classrooms-3110850.

Wormeli, R. (n.d.). *Flexible grouping in the classroom.* https://www.amle.org/
BrowsebyTopic/WhatsNew/WNDet/TabId/270/ArtMID/888/
ArticleID/193/Flexible-Grouping-in-the-Classroom.aspx.

Yale Poorvu Center for Teaching and Learning. (n.d.). *Inclusive teaching strategies.*
Yale University https://poorvucenter.yale.edu/InclusiveTeachingStrategies.

Ziff, B. (n.d.). *Working with the paraprofessional in your classroom. Helpful hints Series
#10.* California State University, Los Angeles. hints10theparaprofessional.
pdf (calstatela.edu)

Zook, C. (2018, October 18). *What is cooperative learning and how does it work?*
Applied Educational Systems. https://www.aeseducation.com/blog/
what-is-cooperative-learning-and-how-does-it-work.

INDEX

ABOUT THE AUTHOR

 Dr. Marlyn Pangatungan is a veteran special education teacher. She moved from the Philippines to the United States in 2008. She serves as a special education lead teacher and a member of the ELA/Math SPED Task Force at her current school. Her education includes an associate degree in information technology, a BA in English, an MA in Montessori education, a Diploma in Special Education, a Reading Specialist Certification, and EdD in transformational leadership.

If you have any question, suggestions, comments or inquiries regarding this book, please contact mpangatungan@yahoo.com.

CPSIA information can be obtained
at www.ICGtesting.com
Printed in the USA
BVHW021504240722
642894BV00020B/443